Phiz!

Phiz!

The Book Illustrations of Hablot Knight Browne

JOHN BUCHANAN-BROWN

To Roberta
from Theo
Christmas 1978

David & Charles
Newton Abbot London Vancouver

British Library Cataloguing in Publication Data
Browne, Hablot Knight
Phiz!
1. Browne, Hablot Knight
I. Buchanan-Brown, John
741.9'42 NC978.5.B'

ISBN 0-7153-7507-5

Text set in Bembo
and printed in Great Britain
by Latimer Trend & Company Limited
Plates printed by Biddles Limited Guildford
for David & Charles (Publishers) Limited
Brunel House Newton Abbot Devon

Published in Canada
by Douglas David & Charles Limited
1875 Welch Street North Vancouver BC

Contents

Acknowledgements

This book could not have been compiled without access to the resources of the British Library (Reference Division) and the Department of Prints and Drawings of the British Museum, most of the plates being reproduced from materials in their possession. My thanks are therefore due to the Trustees of the British Museum for permission to reproduce, from the Department of Prints and Drawings, Plates 10, 15, 24, 31, 86, 88, 90, 96, 98, 102, 124 and 207–9; and to the Director of the British Library (Reference Division) for permission to reproduce all plates other than these and Plates 4–9, 11–14, 16, 20–3, 25–8, 32–43, 69–80, 87, 89, 91, 97, 99–101, 103–13, 117–18, 133–7, 140–7, 152–8, 169–79 and 182–8.

I should like to acknowledge the assistance received from the staffs of both departments and in particular to express my very sincere thanks to the staff of the North Library. The task of examining large numbers of printed books would have been impossible without their help, which is deeply appreciated and for which this is a most inadequate acknowledgement.

I am also grateful to the Dickens Fellowship and to the Victoria and Albert Museum for access to materials in their possession.

Finally I would like to thank the Brighton Public Library and the Hammersmith Reference Library for the loan of books and the staff of the Littlehampton Public Library for obtaining them for me and for their unavailing attempts to obtain other books for me through the public library system.

J.B.-B.

Preface

Hablot Knight Browne ('Phiz') was so productive an artist that a book of this length could not begin to do justice to every side of his talents. I have accordingly confined myself to a brief study of the largest, the most important and the most enduring aspect of his work—his book-illustration—excluding his illustrations in periodicals, his watercolours, sketches and oils. The Introduction provides in continuous narrative a commentary upon the 217 examples of this work reproduced in the Plates and attempts to supply the critical and biographical essentials to their study. I have only departed to some extent from this laconic approach when discussing Browne's designs for wood-engraving, where I feel he labours under a slight injustice. I cannot therefore claim to give anything more than a bare and hardly adequate outline of Phiz's life and work and would refer those who wish to know more about both to my own sources. They are:

E. G. Kitton: *Hablot Knight Browne ('Phiz'). A Memoir* (1882), an extended obituary notice of 32 pages. It prints a number of Browne's letters decorated with his characteristic marginal sketches. (Kitton's *Memoir*.)

David Croal Thomson: *The Life and Labours of Hablot Knight Browne* (1884), the standard work and only full-scale study on the artist. It suffers slightly from the author's lack of sympathy with his subject's way of life (and to a lesser degree with his art), but it does cover every aspect of that art (including watercolours and oils) and contains many reproductions. (Thomson.)

Phiz and Dickens as they appeared to Edgar Browne (1913), a most engaging biographical study of the artist as seen through the eyes of his doctor son and a delightful evocation of a mid-Victorian boyhood. It is illustrated by many examples of Phiz's watercolours, several reproduced in colour.

A large proportion of all these books is devoted to Browne's relations with Dickens and this is the theme of the relevant chapters in F. G. Kitton's *Dickens and his Illustrators* (1899), which also contains biographical matterial not found elsewhere. However, Kitton was writing with the Dickens-collector in mind and both he and the other biographers are mainly descriptive. The two modern sources which best analyse the association are:

John R. Harvey: *Victorian Novelists and their Illustrators* (1970), a full and excellent account, with the advantage of the wider theme to set Browne's work in context. (Harvey.)

Q. D. Leavis: 'The Dickens Illustrations: Their Function' (Chapter VII in F. R. and Q. D. Leavis' *Dickens the Novelist* (1970)), which succinctly penetrates to the core of this relationship. (Mrs Leavis.)

Finally, and although it does not reproduce all but merely the variant Dickens plates, there is:

Albert Johannsen: *Phiz: Illustrations from the Novels of Charles Dickens* (1956), which apart from being a repository of plates contains a great deal of information about their publication and relates them to Browne's other work. (Johannsen.)

I have presented the plates in this book in chronological order and have added a check list of books illustrated by Browne. This is based upon the British Library's *Catalogue* *of Printed Books*, upon the list given by Thomson and references from other sources, notably Kitton's *Memoir*, with such additions as my own researches have provided. It does not pretend to be complete. In it I have noted with an asterisk (*) those books which contain woodcuts, but have not distinguished between those (generally published before 1850) which contain etchings as well, and those (generally after that date) which are wholly illustrated by wood-engraving. Similarly the sign (†) simply indicates a book which contains Browne's work along with that of other illustrators and does not distinguish between a substantial contribution and merely one or two plates by Browne.

J.B.-B.

Introduction

The reputation of Hablot Knight Browne as a book-illustrator has suffered on two counts. On the one hand (and paradoxically) his very success as the illustrator of Dickens has worked against him, for so perfectly did he convey the novelist's purpose in his etchings (an edition illustrated by any other than he is unthinkable) that his personality has become completely sunk in that of Dickens. His pseudonym 'Phiz' was taken to complement Dickens' 'Boz', but Boz has absorbed Phiz and the work of the illustrator has become the province not of the art critic but of the literary critic and more specifically of the Dickens scholar.

On the other hand Browne belongs to a school and a period which has been largely and unjustly ignored by British bibliographers and historians of the illustrated book. The period runs roughly from 1820 to 1860 and it produced what the French have termed the *livre romantique*.[1] Its style is characterized by the extensive use of woodcuts (generally integrated with the text) and by a reflection in the design of the printed page and in the illustrations themselves of the essential elements of literary romanticism. Thus the Gothic and Exotic (particularly Oriental) strains produce imitations, adaptations and developments of the decorated initials and page-borders of medieval and Renaissance manuscripts of both East and West. Similarly the romantic rejection of classical restraint can be seen in the subject-matter of the illustrations and in a fascination with the comic, the macabre and the seamier side of life, realistically and not idealistically depicted. In this respect Browne is very much a romantic artist and an appreciation of his work enables a better understanding of the period and school to which he belongs.

Hablot Knight Browne was born on 12 July 1815 of a family descended from Huguenot refugees who had settled in East Anglia in the seventeenth century and had anglicized their name. They seem to have been of sound middle-class stock, the only evidence of any hereditary artistic talent being afforded by a grandfather, a country clergyman with a taste for antiquities and a talent for water-colour. William Loder Browne (the father) had married the daughter of a Colonel Hunter; Hablot Knight was their ninth son (they thought of calling him Nonus) and thirteenth of their fourteen children. He was christened Hablot[2] in memory of a French officer to whom one of his sisters had been engaged and who had been killed at Waterloo a month before the birth of the artist. Waterloo ended the long war with France and, in the economic slump which followed, the family finances appear to have been seriously embarrassed. Browne's father died abroad in 1823 and his mother lived for many years at St Omer, cheap living on the Continent being the recourse of English gentlefolk in reduced circumstances.

Meanwhile Browne was sent to school at Botesdale in Suffolk, where he was lucky enough to have in the Reverend William Haddock a master who encouraged his artistic bent and for whom he retained a lifelong affection. When he came to leave school he was able to put these talents to good use. His brother-in-law, Elkanan Bicknell,[3] was instrumental in placing Browne as an apprentice with the engraver, Finden, and paid for his indentures. Here, apart from technical training, he received a standard and basic grounding in draughtsmanship, copying and drawing from casts; clearly he put his apprenticeship to good use.

His biographers, however, tend to depict him as the idle apprentice. David Croal Thomson,[4] clearly shocked by Browne's later and somewhat Bohemian attitude towards money and ever ready to point the stern finger of financial rectitude, describes the young Browne as spending more time reading Shakespeare, Smollett and Butler than in engraving blocks—and, when he did, of cutting his own caricatures in the margins. F. G. Kitton,[5] a much more sympathetic witness, probably depicts the young apprentice far more accurately in this story:

> Finding Browne very painstaking and conscientious, his master usually sent him with engraved plates to the printer, in order that he might superintend the operation of proof-taking. As printers usually take their own time over such matters, the youth found that this waiting the pressman's pleasure tried his patience too much. It therefore occurred to him that to spend the interval in the British Museum, hard by, would be much more suited to his tastes. On his returning with the proofs, Finden would praise the boy's diligence, little thinking what trick had been practised on him.

Bearing in mind that when the family had lived in Euston Square, Browne as a schoolboy had been used to visiting the British Museum to draw the Elgin Marbles, a rather different construction may be put upon the story. The facts would seem to be that Browne worked hard enough at his engraving to satisfy Finden and took every opportunity to develop his skill as an artist, since presumably he visited the Museum as an apprentice from motives similar to those which had taken him there as a schoolboy. It seems more likely, too, that it was the industrious rather than the idle apprentice who, in 1833 at the age of eighteen, was awarded the Isis Medal of the Society of Arts for his engraving of John Gilpin's ride. In the following year the young man decided that his real talent lay not in engraving other men's designs but in etching designs of his own or preparing them for other men to engrave. At this early stage in his career he must have shown sufficient promise for so discerning a judge of art as Bicknell to agree to buy him out of his indentures while they had still two years to run.

In 1834, then, he set up in business at No 3 Furnivall's Inn (not far from Dickens at No 15) with his fellow-apprentice, Robert Young, who had just completed his time with Finden. The partnership aimed to work as engravers and etchers, the bulk of this work falling to Young, while Browne was to contribute his share by the production and sale of watercolours.[6] Nor was theirs a hopeless enterprise: apart from the straightforward engraving which their contacts with the trade would undoubtedly bring in, Browne must have impressed his abilities upon influential members of Finden's staff and notably upon Henry Winkles, who now gave Browne his first commission as a book-illustrator in the three-volume *Cathedral Churches of England and Wales* which he planned to publish.

It is hard to say how much of Browne's work for the book is completely original: the generally accepted view is that he simply worked up other men's sketches into finished drawings for the engravers. However, the plates themselves give his name as artist and it is quite possible that the views of St Paul's (e.g., Plate 2) are entirely his. In any event no less than twenty-five of the sixty-one plates in the first volume published in 1836 are attributed to Browne. The number then falls to a mere nine of the fifty-nine plates in Volume II (1838) and to none at all in the third volume. This is understandable, since in 1836 he had begun his real work as an illustrator with *Pickwick* and must have lacked the time even if he had the inclination to continue the collaboration. Nevertheless this commission must have been invaluable in helping to launch the partnership.

Perhaps of more consequence was the support of Finden's manager, J. G. Fennell. It was through him that arrangements had been made to cancel Browne's indentures, and he seems to have helped his ex-apprentice by selling his early watercolours to the art-publisher Adolphus Ackerman. In later life he claimed that it was his suggestion that

Browne should copy Buss' etching 'The Cricket Match' for him to show to Frederick Chapman, thereby obtaining the *Pickwick* commission. However, the truth of the matter is that Chapman, probably impressed by the Gilpin engraving, had already approached the young artist to supply the designs for the woodcuts to illustrate Dickens' squib, *Sunday Under Three Heads*, which Chapman published anonymously in 1836. Browne was then engaged, as successor to Seymour and Buss, to provide designs for the woodcut illustrations in Chapman's short-lived periodical *The Library of Fiction*, comprising one signed and perhaps some eight others.[7] Thus it seems almost natural that, having succeeded Seymour and Buss as house-illustrator on Chapman's periodical, Browne should take over the illustration of *Pickwick* when the death of the first and the manifest in capacity of the second artist caused a crisis in the part-publication of Dickens' first novel.

Despite the competition for the task, perhaps it was Browne's availability which decided the issue, although undoubtedly Dickens' own preferences must have had a very considerable, if not decisive, influence. He must have realized that here was a golden opportunity to turn the tables and to ensure that, from now on, instead of the author providing letterpress for the artist, here would be an artist who would provide plates which would elucidate and reinforce the author's message. Browne was a competent artist; he was at the start of his career; he was two years younger than the novelist, and he must have given evidence of that shyness and modesty which in later years made his contemporaries regard him as something of a recluse. Clearly Browne suited Dickens' purpose far better than the established and greater man, George Cruikshank, who had illustrated Dickens' first book, *Sketches by Boz*, and was to illustrate his next novel, *Oliver Twist*, but who was far too strong and individual a character to fill the rôle which Dickens designed for his illustrators, a rôle so admirably played by Browne.

So he was given the commission and the story goes that an unsuccessful applicant, no less than Thackeray, came round to Furnivall's Inn with the good news and that the pair went off to celebrate and condole over sausages and mash and tankards of beer. Nor was Dickens dissatisfied with the choice: apart from the tribute paid to the artist in the Preface of *Pickwick Papers*, and the acknowledgement of the difficulties under which he had worked ('the greater portion of the illustrations have been executed by the artist from the author's mere verbal description of what he intended to write'), there is the letter which Dickens wrote to John Leech, probably in the summer of 1836, gently but firmly refusing his offer to illustrate *Pickwick* and returning his specimen design, since 'the plates for the Pickwick Papers are in the hands of a gentleman of very great ability, with whose designs I am exceedingly well satisfied, and from whom I feel it neither my wish nor my interest to part'.[8] In fact the partnership was one of the greatest mutual benefit. Contemporary evidence makes it clear that only with the fourth number (the first to be illustrated by Browne) did the novel make any impact and that from then on it gathered momentum. If *Pickwick* set up Dickens as an up-and-coming young novelist, it also established Browne as an illustrator to be sought after.

Since he had inherited to some extent the mantle of Seymour, and Seymour was a sporting artist, it is not unexpected that Browne should have been asked to provide the plates for Surtees' first novel, *Jorrocks' Jaunts and Jollities*, published in 1838. Although John Leech was to make the generous admission that he wished he could draw horses as well as his friend, the illustrations to *Jorrocks* are not among Browne's best work, neither are the plates to *Hawbuck Grange* (1847), and, although the ten which he supplied for *Mr Romford's Hounds* in 1865, when Leech died before completing the series, are of neccessity imitations, they are somewhat pale imitations of the artist who is so firmly associated with Surtees. However, Browne was on the point of forming a far more enduring partnership with a novelist with whom he was to associated for the next thirty years.

Charles Lever was an exceeding prolific writer who enjoyed a wide popularity in his own day, the pink covers of the monthly parts of his novels rivalling the yellows of Thackeray and the greens of Dickens. He was an Irishman who wrote about his countrymen, and his readers thoroughly relished the wealth of incident with which his books were packed and the inexhaustible fund of stories with which they were filled. This is perhaps the clue to his later neglect, since neither compensates for the somewhat perfunctory plotting and characterization of his novels, however good the subjects they were to provide for Browne.

But this was for the future; in 1838 Lever, too, was at the beginning of his career. Born in Dublin in 1806, he had studied medicine at Trinity College, travelled in Germany in 1828 and to Canada in 1829, before qualifying in 1831. He practised at Portstewart in the North and had shown both skill and courage in the cholera epidemic of 1832. His marriage in that year and the consequent need to increase his income, coupled with the stifling atmosphere of a small seaside town, persuaded Lever to enlarge his horizons, and in 1837 he moved to Brussels. As physician to the British Ambassador he was assured not merely of a lucrative practice among the many visitors and the large resident British colony in the Belgian capital but also of the social life which he so much enjoyed.

While at Portstewart he had begun to contribute to *The Dublin University Magazine* and before he left for Belgium he had started his first novel, *Harry Lorrequer*. This had now been accepted by the Dublin publisher, Curry, and in November 1838 Lever wrote from Brussels to Alexander Spencer, the friend who was managing his affairs in Dublin, that one of the partners, James M'Glashan, 'proposes . . . to publish H[arry] L[orrequer] in monthly numbers, with illustrations like the "Pickwick" '. When it emerged that the proposed illustrations were not merely to be 'like the "Pickwick" ' but by the Pickwick artist, Lever was moved to write to Spencer a month later objecting that he 'was very desirous that the illustrations should be by Cruikshank, not Phiz. Pray try to accomplish this for me.' However, Spencer's efforts were unavailing and M'Glashan adamant, so from this apparently unpromising start began the friendly collaboration which was to last until 1865.

With Lever in Brussels, it was with the greater novelist, Charles Dickens, that Browne now became very closely connected. In February author and artist undertook a Yorkshire tour to gather material for *Nicholas Nickleby*; together they visited the Midlands and at the end of the year travelled the Welsh Marches. Both were present in November 1838 at the dinner given in Manchester in Dickens' honour at which he met the prototypes for the Cheeryble Brothers. William Harrison Ainsworth was one of the promoters of the dinner and the occasion bore fruit for Browne in the illustrations he was later to provide for Ainsworth's own novels and the works serialized in *Ainsworth's Magazine*. The relationship between Dickens and Browne as travelling-companions was strengthened on a social level after their return to London from their tours. Dickens' diary from 1837–9 has many references to Browne dining with him, visiting Newgate (25 June 1837), viewing the smouldering ruins of the old Royal Exchange (11 January 1838) or making up parties to Greenwich, and in 1838 Dickens gave his illustrator a valuable cameo ring for Christmas. Of course, Browne had been a guest at the Pickwick dinner of 18 October 1837 and naturally he attended the dinner given on 5 October 1839 to mark the publication of *Nicholas Nickleby*. Since that novel in some sense marks the end of the first phase of Browne's development as an illustrator, this would seem an appropriate point at which to turn for a moment from his life to his art.

The nineteenth-century book-illustrator had at his disposal the three classic printing processes.

There was the planographic—lithography, discovered by Sennenfelder in 1796, by which an artist could draw directly upon a specially treated stone or other surface from which the illustration was to be printed. Only at the very end of his career, however, did Browne work in this medium and it may be ignored for all practical purposes when considering his work.

Then there was the relief process—wood-engraving—in which the artist draws his design directly upon a block of wood for the craftsman—the engraver—to cut away all those portions of the drawing which will be white in the finished print. The raised portions are then inked to leave a black image when impressed upon paper. This was the process used for book-illustration in the fifteenth and sixteenth centuries. It fell into disuse thereafter, except for cheap publications, ornaments and chap-books, until its revival in England at the end of the eighteenth century, when it superseded, or at any rate competed upon equal terms with, the process which had suceeded the woodcut in the seventeenth century—the intaglio.

Intaglio is the reverse of the relief process. In other words, instead of the raised surface of the block being the printing surface, it is the recessed area of a metal plate. This is either cut out with a burin (engraving) or eaten away with acid (etching). The block is inked and the ink wiped off the raised surface. The ink remaining in the recesses of the block is then impressed upon paper by a special press able to exert the great pressure required to transfer the image to the paper.

The extensive use of the woodcut as a medium of book-illustration in this, the Romantic period, arises from the proven ability of Bewick and the engravers who succeeded him to achieve in the far less tractable material of wood the same delicacy of line as the copper-plate engraver. Had this skill not been demonstrated in such consciously fine books as, say, the Goldsmith issued by the famous press of William Bulmer in 1796 with Bewick's woodcuts, the economic advantage of the woodcut would not have been applied to the better class of illustrated book. This advantage lay in the fact that, since the woodcut is a relief process, text and illustrations can be printed together at one pull of the press, whereas the intaglio process requires either separate plates to be printed or, where text and illustration are integrated, for the sheets to be run for a second time through a special press. To this economic advantage, the woodcut added the aesthetic advantage of providing a sharper image than the copperplate, and this harmonized better with the brilliant typography of the period. However, from the mid-1820s the newly-invented steel-engraving, with its image sharper than the old copperplate, returned as a process of illustration, even in integrated books where the cost-saving of the relief process was not a crucial factor.

It should therefore be stressed that at the start of Browne's career the relief and intaglio processes were alternative methods of reproducing what was essentially the same sort of design. Thus Browne asks the engraver of such early woodcuts as the frontispiece to *Sunday Under Three Heads* (Plate 3(a)) or 'The Dying Beggar' (Plate 3(b)) to achieve precisely the same effect of dense engraving and delicate miniature which he himself obtains in such etchings as 'The Manly Young Lady' or 'The Poetical Young Gentleman' (Plates 17(a) and (b)). Of course Browne was fortunate in being able to entrust his designs to a group of engravers of unsurpassed virtuosity—Landells, Gray, Williams and others—whose members exported themselves and their skills to Europe. The ability of the engraver to interpret Browne's designs is a crucial factor in any assessment of the value of Browne's work in this medium, but for the moment I would merely remark that while the designs for *Morals from the Churchyard* (1838) exhibit little originality, being agreeable examples of the decorative vignette of the period 1800–30, the woodcuts in *Sunday Under Three Heads* (1836) and *The Handbook of Swindling* (1839) share the same characteristics as his etched work and are just as much a product of his technical and artistic training in that medium.

By comparison with his successors in the 1860s, Browne seems almost self-taught. That his Suffolk schoolmaster encouraged his artistic leanings as a boy would imply that he received such teaching as was then and there available; and, as we know, his apprenticeship to Finden comprised training in draughtsmanship as well as engraving. In addition he is known to have attended the art school in St Martin's Lane put by Thackeray into *The Newcomes* under the name of Gandish's and which, if we are to believe Thackeray, was a somewhat haphazard and happy-go-lucky establishment which may have polished a talent being developed in Finden's engraving studio. Indeed, the strongest characteristic of Browne's early work is the revelation of the craft which he had learned from Finden. This is pre-eminently the skill of the miniaturist which can be seen in such a wide variety of illustration of the period. It ranges from the detail of full-page architectural and topographical plates, of which Browne's own view of St Paul's (Plate 2) might be an example, to the delicacy of the vignettes which really require a magnifying-glass to discover all their subtleties, subtleties which can often be missed in appreciating the general decorative effect which a head- or tail-piece gives to the printed page.

This training, this skill in etching in miniature, is, then, the characteristic of the early series of plates for *Pickwick*, for *Nicholas Nickleby* and for *Harry Lorrequer* where, even when he has the larger octavo page at his disposal, the artist seems reluctant to break from the miniature mould. This results in a certain cramped, stiff feeling in his figures and a loss of dramatic impact when he has to depict a crowd scene. This is particularly noticeable when he shows Nicholas paying Squeers in his own coin (Plate 22), where the drama is lost in a jumble of tiny figures. This is perhaps an extreme case, since the composition is not of the strongest, but even in better-balanced plates such as 'The Internal Economy of Dotheboys Hall' (Plate 21) or 'The Election of Eatanswill' (Plate 6) a great deal of the effect is lost because the fine detail of facial expression is hardly visible to the naked eye.

When the plate is less crowded, the somewhat small scale does not prevent effective character drawing. The contrasts between the honest countenance of Mr Pickwick and the sly, sniggering clerks in 'Mr Pickwick and Sam in the Attorney's Office' (Plate 7), the nice mixture of emotions on the faces of all the characters in 'Mrs Bardell encounters Mr Pickwick in the Prison' (Plate 13), or the look of horror on Mr Pickwick's face and the blissful ignorance of the middle-aged lady (Plate 8) all show Browne's lively sense of the dramatic or the ridiculous and his ability to convey it in facial expression.

Choice of subject-matter was, of course, to a greater or lesser degree in the hands of the author (Dickens from the first preserved a tight control), but through Browne's earlier work there runs a thread of boyish delight in slapstick. Typical are the two plates (29 and 30) from *Harry Lorrequer* which made Charles Lever complain that it was the illustrations which unfairly branded his novels as uproarious.[9] Yet the same spirit may be seen in *Pickwick* in, for example, 'The Election at Eatanswill', 'Bob Sawyers' Mode of Travelling' (Plate 14) or 'The Rival Editors' (Plate 16). They are typical of the Browne who accompanied Dickens to the theatre at Shrewsbury during their Welsh tour in 1838 and then 'laughed with such indecent heartiness at one point of the entertainments that an old gentleman in the next box suffered the most violent indignation'. The same Browne could depict in knockabout terms the farcial interruption of high tragedy at the Royal Victoria by the orange-seller walking on stage. How very unlike the theatre's old age, as the Old Vic, but it was next door to the New Cut, one of the most notorious slums in Victorian London, full of the low-life characters, pickpockets and all, which Browne so lovingly depicts in the foreground of 'A Scene before the Curtain' (Plate 18).

There are, however, signs of the way in which Browne's art was to develop. 'Mr Wardle and his Friends under the Influence of Salmon' (Plate 4) shows a deeper comic spirit in the nicely contrasted expressions of the tipsy Pickwickians—Browne has a good eye for a drunk—their horrified hosts and the delighted domestics, but it is one or two of the *Nickleby* plates which foreshadow a greater freedom. In 'Theatrical Emotion of Mr Vincent Crummles' (Plate 23) Browne seems to be breaking away from the cramped confines of the vignette plate and to be more ready to fill the page with his design.

Yet, oddly enough for those who maintain that Browne could not design for wood-engraving, it is in the woodcuts for Dickens' *Master Humphrey's Clock* (1840–1) that he inaugurated a decade containing his best and most characteristic work. This includes the illustrations to three more novels by Dickens, *Martin Chuzzlewit* (1843), *Dombey and Son* (1848) and *David Copperfield* (1850); Lever's *Jack Hinton the Guardsman* (*Our Mess* I: 1843), *The O'Donoghue* (1845), *The Knight of Gwynne* (1847), *The Confessions of Con Cregan* (1849) and *Roland Cashel* (1850); and a notable series of illustrations for such other novels as W. J. Neale's *Paul Periwinkle* (1841), Thomas Miller's *Godfrey Malvern* (1842), Ainsworth's *Revelations to London* (1844–5), W. B. Jerrold's *The Disgrace to the Family* (1848) and the Mayhews' *The Image of his Father* (1849). The immediate impression that they give is one of confidence, a confidence which fills the page so that the vignette plate ceases to be merely the vignette and becomes more truly a plate. It is a confidence, too, which reveals itself in the sure handling of movement, whether it is the mass of struggling figures in 'The Collision with the Prosperity' (Plate 52), the dramatic incident of 'The Rescue' (Plate 48), or the highly successful 'The Prosperity going down' (Plate 53), so full of the howling gale and the tossing seas.

Furthermore, Browne shows a taste for and a mastery of the grotesque, the sinister and the macabre, demonstrated earlier in his 'The Goblin and the Sexton' (Plate 9). All these elements are present in his designs for *Master Humphrey's Clock*, and in particular in the character of the dwarf, Quilp. How well Browne convey's his malevolence (Plates 33 and 35) and how splendidly macabre are the lonely marshes with Quilp's corpse left stranded by the falling tide (Plate 39). This same mastery of the macabre comes over in 'The Irish Wake (Plate 46), with the body of the hanged man jerking upright in his coffin as the donkey-cart bounces over the rough track away from the gallows. How well, too, can Browne convey the sinister, as in 'The Compact' (Plate 82), or the menacing, whether it is Mr Gashford, perched like some bird of prey on the leads of his house (Plate 42), or the threatening mounted figure of Mr Darius (Plate 61).

We have seen how Browne uses the grotesque to convey fear and horror, but he can also make you feel his enjoyment of the grotesque for its own sake, as in the Marchioness and the Jolly Sandboys in the *Old Curiosity Shop* (Plates 34 and 38), or in, Cornelius O' Dowd (Plate 63). There is too, a more genuine humour, less forced than the more obviously farcical aspects of his earlier work, expressed in the shocked bewilderment of the Hackney Coachman being robbed by John Smith (Plate 45), in the effrontery of the street arab, Con Cregan, taking his chop in Kileen's fashionable dining-room (Plate 128) or in the sheer impudence depicted in Plates 121 and 122, from *The Image of his Father*. But Browne needed strong characters to demonstrate his capacity, whether they were Neale's Admiral Blowhard (Plate 50), Gregory Gruff (Plate 58) or Mrs Grumblebum (Plate 114), and his success with these creations of minor novelists becomes all the more marked when he was illustrating a writer of genius. Because his Pecksniff (Plates 69, 72, 80) and his Micawber (Plates 141, 144, 147) are such masterpieces of humourous draughtsmanship there is the temptation to concentrate upon these comic characters and to ignore Browne's more serious work, the masterly portrait of Hugh in *Barnaby Rudge* (Plate 40), the confident handling of Tipperary Joe (Plate 65), the strength with which he depicts old Martin Chuzzlewit (Plates 70 and 79) and the way in which he progresses from the sentimentality of Plate 28 to the genuine sentiment of such *Copperfield* plates as 'Changes at Home' (135) or 'Martha' (142).

If these aspects of his work show how Browne's artistic self-confidence blossomed in the 1840s, it is perhaps his approach to the problems of light and shade and in particular his handling of night scenes which best demonstrate his growing competence and foreshadow his later etching techniques. At the outset he relied on a *trompe-l'oeil* for this effect. Thus, in the night-scene 'Mr Winkle's Situation when the Door blew to' (Plate 12), the eye accepts what is really a negative as a positive image. In other words, the figures of Mr Winkle himself, the chairmen and the lady revealed by the flickering torch-light are the most heavily etched and therefore the blackest; the background is lightly etched so that the fading into imperceptibility of the building and of the faces at the windows, which is actually the effect of darkness, is here achieved by grey and white areas. Although the eye transforms this, it is an unsatisfactory solution and Browne gradually evolved different techniques to obtain the effects which he desired. Initially darkness and pools of shadow could be portrayed by freehand lines more or less densely and more or less deeply etched. This is not always entirely successful—'Smith stabbing a Policeman' (Plate 47) and 'The Consultation in the Devil's Cavern' (Plate 51) are examples—but at its best it is capable of such impressive plates as the series of beside scenes in *Godfrey Malvern*, *Tom Burke* and *Martin Chuzzlewit* (Plates 58, 66, 70); 'Pinch starts Homeward with the new Pupil' (Plate 71), with the trap emerging from the shadow of the arch into the sunlight; 'Martin meets an Acquaintance . . .' (Plate 73); and 'The River' (Plate 146).

The technique chosen for this last plate is interesting since it is a subject which would seem to demand treatment in a style which Browne had by now begun to develop—the so-called 'dark' plate. In these dark plates Browne uses a ruling-machine to obtain dense masses of black and to give the steel-etching almost the effect of a mezzotint. It was a technique he was to employ far more widely in the 1850s, but early examples include 'On the dark Road' from *Dombey and Son* (1848), 'The Ganger's Fate' from *The Pottleton Legacy* (1849) and a number of illustrations of *Roland Cashel* (1850), of which perhaps the most effective is 'The Game at Monte' (Plates 108, 132, 148). It seems very probable that Browne received the hint from John Franklin, who had used the technique for his illustrations to the part-issues of Ainsworth's *Old St Paul's*. When the novel was issued as a bound volume in 1847, Browne provided a vignette title and a frontispiece—'The Carouse of the Coffin-makers'—but the latter, with its conventional hatching, markedly fails to achieve the sinister effect of Franklin's dark, not to say black, plates.

At the same time Browne was also experimenting with another technique which allowed the steel-etching to achieve the effects of a pen-and-wash drawing. This can be very effective when the 'pen' lines are firm and the composition itself is strong, as in the case of 'The Money Lender' (Plate 149), but it does tend to accentuate any weakness of line and composition and to give the overall wishy-washy appearance of so many of the plates in Lever's later novels. 'A Domestic Detective' (Plate 150) is a good example of a bad plate. This wash effect was achieved by very shallow etching in which a thin film, rather than a deposit of ink, would gather to be impressed on the paper.

In the realization of these special techniques, as indeed in straightforward etching, an essential rôle was played by Browne's partner, Robert Young. At the start of their association Browne had been primarily the designer and watercolourist, putting his share into the kitty from the sale of these originals. Young was the engraver and etcher and this he remained even when the bulk of Browne's output comprised etchings on steel-plates.

Etching is, however, a lengthy process; first the design has to be transferred to the specially waxed surface of the plate, then the etcher must use his needle to cut through the wax and onto or into the plate and finally the black image must be 'bitten-in' to the plate by subjecting it to a solution of acid. Since the depth of etching governs the degree of blackness of this image—normally perspective is indicated by progressively deeper etching from background to foreground—variation in depth of etching is achieved by coating or 'stopping-out' an area with varnish once it has been etched to the necessary depth.

We shall see that the pressures under which Browne worked would have made it physically impossible for him to have carried through all these stages in etching single-handed, and this is where Young came in, for he undertook the 'biting-in' of the plates. Such work demanded close understanding between partners and detailed instructions on Browne's part, as evidence from the early days of their partnership shows. In the copy of *Sketches of Young Ladies*, once in the Suzannet Collection and now in the Library of the Dickens Fellowship, are bound, as extra illustrations, the set of Browne's original roughs. A number of these carry his instructions to Young. For example, the sketch for 'The Manly Lady'—the finished etching is Plate 17(a)—has Browne's notes: 'Put a rebating ground so that I may etch the head. HKB' and 'Stop out the young lady's hat & tail.' The first instruction shows that Browne needed to correct an error, the second that Young must be prevented from compounding the error by biting it in still further. Finally the plates would be returned to the artist for retouching where necessary, as an instruction on another sketch indicates: 'Bite the face of the girl between the old women *slightly*—& let me have it back to touch upon. HKB'

Notwithstanding the part played by Young, etching was a most intimate process in which the artist was directly involved with the medium by which his designs were reproduced. Unlike the originals passed to an engraver and which so often lose some of their spontaneity in their passage to the block, the surviving roughs of Browne's illustrations are lifeless by comparison with the etchings themselves. Dickens is something of a special case and I suspect the sketches for him were more detailed than those for, say, Charles Lever, but even the study for 'The Rival Editors' (Plate 15) shares the characteristics of the set of roughs for *The O'Donoghue*, in that it is far more of an overall indicator of the position of characters in the scene designated for illustration than in any sense an exact prefiguration of the finished plate. However, the best evidence for the verve which came from the etcher's needle is provided by comparison of three of *The O'Donoghue* roughs (Plates 86, 88, 90) with the respective etchings (Plates 87, 89, 91).

Admittedly, drawings made with a soft pencil are bound to suffer a certain loss of detail over the years, but in these instances it may be less than one might expect, since the physical and particularly the facial characteristics of the characters had been predetermined by author and artist. Examples of this sort of study of a minor character are provided by the sketches for the Cheeryble Brothers (Plate 24) or Mr Weller Senior (Plate 10). When a more important character was concerned there were bound to be difficulties, as for example with Mr Dombey in *Dombey and Son*. Here there were additional complications because Dickens was living in Lausanne and, although Browne sent him a large sheet of studies (part of which is reproduced as Plate 112) on which the novelist marked the heads which came nearest to his visualization so that a composite could be produced, Dickens was not entirely satisfied because now, as on so many other occasions, he had a specific City magnate, in mind.[10] Finally, when minor characters did not rise to the dignity of such separate sheets of studies, they might have an enlargement of their faces sketched in the margin of the rough in which they appeared, and Mrs

Gamp receives this treatment in the study for 'Mrs Gamp propoges a Toast' (finished etching, Plate 78), preserved in the Library of the Dickens Fellowship.

Nor was the provision of illustrations for novels issued in parts a leisurely process. The writer had to produce his copy for Browne to make his roughs to a very tight monthly schedule. We have seen how, in Browne's first commission, *Pickwick*, these pressures were so extreme as to force him to design, not from what Dickens had written, but from what he intended to write; and this need to produce under pressure high-quality work which corresponded exactly with the text remained a constant bugbear. In February 1858, during the serialization of *Mervyn Clitheroe*, Ainsworth had obviously received complaints from Frederick Warne (then working for Routledge, Ainsworth's publisher) that Browne was slow in delivering the plates and that the plates themselves were slapdash. On 14 February he wrote to Browne:

> I do not perceive that the *best* plates were hurried as Mr Warne seems to intimate. They came out extremely well, I think, and are generally liked.
>
> I hope the present subject suits you. 'The Conjurers Interrupted' [Plate 156] will be effective, if I am not mistaken.
>
> Pray tell your plate-maker to send me proofs early (no matter how rough), that I may prevent any variations between the text and the illustrations. And be as early as you conveniently can, to avoid any grumbling on the part of Mr Warne. I suppose he will require to publish on Thursday, 25th.

These problems became all the more acute when author and illustrator were as widely separated as were Browne and Lever for virtually all their working lives. The first novel to be illustrated by Phiz, *Harry Lorrequer*, was written in Brussels and published in Dublin with the artist working in London, and it is apparent from a letter which Lever wrote to his publisher, M'Glashan, on 11 January 1839 that in these circumstances the choice of the passages to be illustrated rested with Browne:

> H. K. Browne has not written to me, and I regret it the more, because if I knew the scenes he selected, I might have benefitted by his ideas and rendered them more graphic as an author corrects his play by seeing a dress rehearsal. . . .

Nor could distance and the pressures of serial publication permit of rough sketches being sent to the author; and here was a further worry for Lever:

> Has Phiz any notion of Irish physiognomy? for this is most important. If not, and as 'Lorrequer' abounds in specimens, pray entreat him to study the Tail[11] when they meet in February: he can have nothing better, if not too coarse, for his purposes.

The difficulties of communicating at a distance are underlined by the fact that not even the diplomatic bag, which Lever as physician to the British Ambassador used to send copy of his publisher, was safe. In January/February 1839 the last instalment of *Harry Lorrequer* went astray, with the result, as Lever wrote to M'Glashan on 16 February, that 'The scenes for illustration are not so good, of course, in the concluding No.'.

However, once the strains of writing were over and *Lorrequer* had been published in volume form, a more relaxed Lever could ask his friend Alexander Spencer: 'Tell me what you think of the illustrations. I am much pleased with them.'

This same letter of April 1839 announces that he has started work on *Charles O'Malley*; once serialization was under way the same problems occurred. On 20 September the harassed novelist was writing to M'Glashan: 'I wish you would suggest scenes to Browne, his choice latterly is not over happy.' The real solution was a meeting between author and artist and, although this was deferred, it eventually took place in September 1841. Browne was accompanied by the Irish poet, Samuel Lover, and the visit was a great success. Lever was an excellent host and in the less than three weeks which they stayed with him, they managed between them to consume some nine dozen bottles of champagne. Nor was business entirely excluded, although Lever was not perhaps quite open with Spencer when he wrote to him on 2 November 1841 that 'Browne (Phiz) has been with us for the last few weeks making arrangements about the illustrations, and I think this part, at least, will be better than heretofore'.

The book in question was *Jack Hinton the Guardsman*, which forms the first volume of *Our Mess*, and, although he complained about them at the time, the illustrations prove that his confidence was not misplaced. They are the most successful which Browne had so far provided for Lever, although how much 'The Finale to an Evening' (Plate 62) owes to Browne's experience of Lever's hospitality had better be left unresolved. Then, in 1842, Lever returned to Ireland to edit *The Dublin University Magazine*, having finally abandoned medicine for writing. Whether it is the blossoming of Browne's talents or the easier communication between artist and illustrator (Browne made the first of two visits to Ireland in 1845), *The O'Donoghue* and *St Patrick's Eve* (both 1845) contain excellent work, maintained in *The Knight of Gwynne* (published in 1847, but begun in 1845 before Lever resigned his editorship and left Ireland for the Tyrol[12]).

While it is clear from the foregoing that both Lever and Ainsworth were concerned that Browne's illustrations should not misrepresent their text, it is equally clear that they conceived the illustrations as having a decorative function, and were in fact quite prepared to alter what they had written to preserve its consistency with what Browne had etched. Dickens, however, had a very different view of the function of illustration and a correspondingly different relationship with Browne from the easy terms of friendship which Browne and Lever enjoyed. In brief, Dickens saw that he was writing for what was virtually a newly-literate public, but a public nurtured upon the visual imagery of the political and moralistic prints of Hogarth and his successors, of whom Browne was one. Unused to the imaginative stimulus of the printed word, but with a long tradition of drawing the 'message' from such pictorial novels as Hogarth's 'Rake's Progress', Dickens' readers would only enjoy his novels and grasp his intentions fully if the plates which the artist provided could be no mere adjunct to but an extension of the written text. In Browne Dickens found the ideal instrument to achieve these aims. Their working relations were very close and the control which the novelist exercised over his artist virtually complete, although to be successful this control had never to degenerate into a tyranny which would deny the willing cooperation of the artist.

This was available for most, at least, of their association. The studies for 'The Dombey Family' (Plate 96) and for 'I make myself known to my Aunt' (Plates 138 and 139) show how Browne was ready to suggest—and Dickens to accept—pictorial effects which conveyed the essence of the scene better than the text with which they were slightly at variance (Mr Dombey was originally described as standing, David's aunt as sitting). And how well did Browne respond to the demands of constant and detail instructions, of which this (contained in a letter from Dickens of 10 March 1845) in his characteristic both of the detailed nature of the novelist's specifications and of their underlying motive:

> The first subject I am now going to give is very important to the book. *I should like to see your sketch of it, if possible.*
>
> I should premise that I want to make the Major, who is the incarnation of selfishness and small revenge, a kind of comic Mephistophilean power in the book; and the No. begins with the departure of Mr Dombey and the Major on that trip for change of air and scene which is prepared for in the last Number. They go to Leamington, where you and I were once. In the Library the Major introduces Mr Dombey to a certain lady, whom, as I wish to foreshadow dimly, said Dombey may come to marry in due season. She is about thirty, not a day more—handsome, though haughty looking—good figure, well dressed, showy, and desirable. Quite a lady in appearance, with something of a

proud indifference about her, suggestive of a spark of the Devil within. Was married young. Husband dead. Goes about with an old mother, who rouges, and who lives upon the reputation of a diamond necklace and her family. Wants a husband. Flies at none but high game, and couldn't marry anybody not rich. Mother affects cordiality and heart, and is the essence of sordid calculation. Mother usually shoved about in a Bath chair by a page who has rather outgrown and outshoved his strength, and who butts at it behind like a ram, while his mistress languidly steers it by a handle in front. Nothing the matter to prevent her walking, only was once when a Beauty sketched reclining in a Barouche, and having outlived the Beauty and the Barouche too, still holds to the attitude as becoming her uncommonly. Mother is in this machine in sketch. Daughter has parasol.

The Major presents them to Mr. Dombey, gloating within himself over what may become of it, and over the discomfiture of Miss Tox. Mr Dombey (in deep mourning) bows solemnly. Daughter bends. The native in attendance, bearing a camp-stool and the Major's greatcoat. Native evidently afraid of the Major and his thick cane. If you like it better, the scene may be in the street or in a green lane. But a great deal will come of it; and I want the Major to express that, as much as possible in the apoplectic Mephistophilean observation of the scene, and his share in it.

Lettering, *Major Bagstock is delighted to have the opportunity.*

Browne duly sent Dickens the sketch (Plate 102) and on 15 March the novelist replied:

> The sketch is admirable; the women *quite perfect.* I cannot tell you how much I like the younger one. There are one or two points, however, which I must ask you to alter. They are captial in themselves, and I speak solely for the story.
>
> First—I grieve to write it—that Native, who is prodigiously good as he is, must be in European costume. He may wear earrings and look outlandish, and be dark brown. [It will be noticed that in the sketch he is partially erased and that the finished etching (Plate 103) is entirely to Dickens' specifications.] In this fashion he must be of Moses, Mosesy. I don't mean Old Testament Moses, but him of the Minories.
>
> Secondly, if you *can* make the Major older, and with a larger face, do.
>
> That's all. Never mind the Pump-room now, unless you have found the sketch, as we may have that another time. I shall propose to you a trip to Leamington together. We might go one day and return the next.

Three things emerge from this exchange. First is the very detailed nature of Dickens' instructions, so minute in every particular that on another occasion when the novelist sent the equally precise specifications for 'The City of Eden . . . in fact' (Plate 75), Browne was moved to comment wryly: 'I can't get all the perspective in—unless you allow of a long subject—something less than a mile.' But this constant limitation of his own artistic imagination, this need to see the scene always through the novelist's eyes and never through his own, must have been a perpetual irritation, however good-humouredly it was borne.

Next, Dickens was often less than whole-hearted in his praise; there must so often have been 'one or two points to alter'. This must have been another source of irritation and all the more galling when Browne, having executed what is artistically a successful plate, such as 'Paul and Mrs Pipchin' (Plate 99), then had it subjected to such criticism on non-artistic grounds as Dickens voiced to John Forster.

> I am really *distressed* by the illustration of Mrs. Pipchin and Paul. It is so frightfully and wildly wide of the mark. Good Heaven! in the commonest and most literal construction of the text it is all wrong. . . . I can't say what pain and vexation it is to be so utterly misrepresented. I would cheerfully have given a hundred pounds to have kept this illustration out of this book.

In fact Browne's crime was not so heinous as Dickens would suggest. He had illustrated the scene as it was written by Dickens but not as he had visualized it. It was, after all, a piece of the novelist's own childhood and all the more precious and vivid for that. But how was the unfortunate artist to know this?

Finally, these notes give some indication of the speed at which Browne had to work. Dickens sent him the original specification on 10 March and yet was able to return the sketch submitted by the artist, with his comments, by 15 March. Allowing for the time taken in the post, this is not bad, yet it is slightly slow by comparison with the turn-round achieved in 1839 for the monthly part of *Nicholas Nickleby* for which Browne provided:

A Diary

Friday, evening, 11th Jan.
Received portion of copy containing Subject No. 1.
Sunday
Posted sketch to Dickens.
Monday evening, 14th Jan.
Received back sketch of Subject No. 1. from Dickens, enclosing a subject for No. 2.
Tuesday, 15th Jan.
Forwarded sketch of Subject 2 to Dickens.
Wednesday, 16th Jan.
Received back ditto.
Sunday
Tuesday, 22 Jan.
First plate finished.
Saturday, 26th Jan.
Second ditto finished.—Supposing that I had nothing else to do, you may see by the foregoing that I could not well commence etching operations until Wednesday, the 16th.

You may date from the receipt of the first sketch back from Dickens	Tuesday	15
		16
		17
		18
		19
	Sunday	20
		21
		22 Plate No. 1 finished
		23
		24
		25
	Saturday	26 Plate No. 2 finished
		—
		10 days

I make ten days to etch and finish four etchings. What do you make of it?

It is extraordinary that, working under such pressure, Browne should have been able to maintain so high a standard. It should also be noticed that in this instance from the two subjects were produced four etchings. This is because, although the etched plates were printed separately from the text, inking and then printing from the steel plates was a comparatively slow process. With a popular author such as Dickens the number of copies to be printed each month was correspondingly high and sufficient plates could not be printed from a single steel in time to satisfy the demand. Hence, at least so far as Dickens was concerned, Browne had to provide two and sometimes three copies of each plate for illustration. Now, if merely the books in my Check List (see page 195) are taken into account—and the list does not pretend to be complete nor does it include periodical work—in the twelve years from 1839 to 1850 Browne not only executed roughly 300 designs for wood-engraving but also supplied over 800 illustrations for etching. In other words he averaged slightly more than five etchings a month throughout this period and, since many must have been etched in duplicate or even triplicate, he must actually have etched something nearer seven or eight plates a month. Hence the need for Robert Young to do the 'biting-in' and hence, too, the somewhat different complexion which may be put upon his move from London in 1846 to Thornton Heath, in Surrey.

In 1840 Browne had married a Miss Reynolds. At first they lived in Howland Street, off the Tottenham Court Road, then at Stamford Villas in the Fulham Road. Browne's biographers attributed the move out of London to the state of Mrs Browne's health and this is, indeed, a very plausible reason. Browne himself came from a large family and by 1878 had nine children living, of whom some were still dependent upon him. Allowing for miscarriages and the infant mortality of the day, his son Edgar's recollection of a regular succession of baby brothers and sisters may not be far out and would explain the move from Mrs Browne's point of view. It may perhaps have suited her husband just as much, if not more, to set a distance between himself and his publishers as to give his wife and healthy surroundings of then-rural Surrey in which to bear and bring up their children. For by now, as we have seen, Browne was a very busy man who had consolidated the reputation made with *Pickwick*. Indeed, he received from D. Appleton & Co of New York a commission in 1842 to illustrate *The Career of Puffer Hopkins*. The results were less than happy as the author, Cornelius Mathews, was to remark in his Preface:

> It will be perceived that a portion of the text is illustrated by H. K. Browne, Esq., (PHIZ) of London. In justice to the artist, it should be added, that the distance, at which he labored, from the author, has caused him to depart, in some particulars, from the conception it was the author's purpose to embody. As they are the first and only designs procured from that gentleman for America, the author ventures to add, that he regards them, with this reservation, as eminently ingenious and spirited.

This is a handsome tribute to competent examples of Browne's work in the period. One has been included as Plate 55, both because of the uniqueness of the commission and because I have a sneaking suspicion that the Brummellian figure of the Master Tailor from Broadway may have made Mathews realize that Phiz was not perhaps the man to embody his conceptions.

Although no further American publishers came knocking at his door, Browne was an extremely popular and sought-after illustrator and, had not his temperament so inclined him, pressure of work might well have driven him from London. His circumstances favoured the move. In Robert Young he had a faithful and dependable partner who was in a very real sense the managing director of their joint enterprise. Quite apart from the work he did biting-in the etchings, he seems to a large degree to have handled the business side, the dealing with publishers and authors, for Edgar Browne remembered him as generally accompanying any business visitors to the house in Croydon, and he must have screened the artist from casual callers.

If the departure from London removed this type of pressure it also enabled Browne to give up the social life which impinged upon his work. This suited his temperament, for, as his son wrote,

> He was by nature shy and given to self-effacement, and when he became a busy man, and had consequently little time or opportunity for social amusement, these tendencies increased till his dread of strangers amounted to a detrimental feature in his character. It became difficult to make him go anywhere . . . if people could be brought to him he was always a cheerful host. . . . But by living so much alone in his studio, having an innate dislike of push, and a sort of natural distrust of strangers, he gradually worked himself up till it was difficult to get him to see anybody but intimate friends.

However, by restricting his social round to chosen friends and by avoiding being lionized by Croydon society, Browne was able to concentrate upon the two things most dear to him, his family and his art.

His son Edgar pays a revealing tribute in this connection when he writes: 'He was in a remarkable degree the centre of the household. My mother adored him, and considered that he could do no wrong. We boys regarded him as our best friend. . . .' Indeed, Edgar's book is in so many respects the evocation of an extremely happy boyhood. The 'Governor' might shut himself away all the morning in his studio, but the children had their friends, their large garden and the still unspoiled Surrey countryside in which to ramble and play. Then, in the afternoon, there was their father to take them riding[13] or picnicking, to interest them in books and reading in the evenings, to take them to London for the theatre and other entertainments or the Crystal Palace for the music and the fireworks and to pack them off to the National Gallery with strict instructions to study David Cox.

Browne's life at Thornton Heath and later at Banstead revolved around his family, and in bringing them up and watching them develop he was able to relax from the strains of his success as an illustrator. His love of children is apparent in some of his *Dombey* plates and more particularly in the illustrations to *David Copperfield*. Although his watercolours are outside the scope of this study, many of them are redolent of the charming, albeit sentimental, middle-class domesticity reflected in his *Home Pictures* (1851), a volume of finely-printed, tinted etchings of which Plates 161–3 are typical examples. His was an eminently productive and happy life, and this lasted until the end of 1859, when changed circumstances forced the family to return to London.

Browne's biographers (including his son) have attributed these circumstances—the fall-off in work and income due to an apparent decline in his abilities—to the Surrey seclusion, to the fact that, since Phiz never drew from models but purely from the imagination,[14] cutting himself off from society cut him off from the sources at which his imagination could recharge its reservoir of images. Perhaps there is some truth in this, but the reasons for this so-called decline are much more complex and have far more to do with the kind of novels being published, the sort of public for which they were intended, the type of illustration which that public expected, the changes in the medium used for book-illustration and a new pattern of publishing fiction.[15]

Most important of all these is undoubtedly the arrival of a new and far more sophisticated class of novel-reader to whom the image created by his or her own reaction to the novelist was stronger and subjectively truer than any image created by the illustrator, however accurately it might embody the novelist's own conception of scene or character. These readers did not, in any case, need the reinforcement of the novelist's message by the Hogarthian imagery of the tackle-shop in the background of Smike's recapture (Plate 26), nor was it necessary that a deserted wife should be depicted (as in Plate 59) with a copy of *Don Juan* lying on the floor and a picture labelled 'The Truant' hanging on the wall. As novelists responded to this new public, illustration became less and less relevant to their work, and remains almost through force of habit. However, the immediate effect upon Lever and Dickens, Browne's principal source of commissions, was to raise the tone of their fictions and to require from their illustrator (in the case of Dickens) that he should convey mood and atmosphere rather than the strong characters and situations of the past.

Moreover, if the new public had grown more sophisticated in its reading habits, it had also become more serious in its appreciation of art. This is the age of Victorian 'High Art' reflected in book-illustration by the style known as 'The 'Sixties Book'. Inaugurated by William Allingham's *The Music Master* (1855), it is in some sense the triumph of the German-inspired stream of Romantic art, with its high-minded idealization of the human figure and its Nazarene simplicity, and a revulsion from the Franco-British stream, with its realism, its elaboration and its penchant for the comic and the grotesque.

Browne reacted to the new taste which preferred a prettified Marchioness (Plate 110) to the more realistic woodcut (Plate 38) with the 'Book of Beauty' style of the extra illustrations to *Barnaby Rudge* and *Dombey and Son* (Plates 111, 124, 125,), and to the need to convey atmosphere rather than incident by no radical change in his style but by developing further techniques which he had already employed. Thus he tends to simplify his etching on the one hand, using a line unsupported by hatching, and on the other increasingly to use 'stopping-out' to achieve the effect of a pen-and-wash drawing, both these concurrently with a far higher proportion of his atmospheric 'dark' plates. Perhaps because the novels themselves were moving away from the need for specific illustration, these dark plates are the best things which Browne produced during what may be termed his second period, roughly between 1850 and 1860.

By controlling the depth of the etching

he was able to produce striking effects, from the sinister darkness of many of the *Bleak House* plates (175–9) or of those for *Mervyn Clitheroe* (Plates 154–7), to the chilly black of 'Little Dorrit's Party' (Plate 184) and the even more effective 'The Asylum for the Houseless' (Plate 189). What is more, by combining 'wash' with 'dark' plate effects, as in 'Making Off' (Plate 182), or on its own, as in 'The Ferry' (Plate 185), Browne could create the illusion of sunlight and shadow or of pure sunlight. By and large, however, and as we have seen in the case of *The Daltons*, the wash effect tends to be wishy-washy. The line loses strength and, although Browne produced perfectly competent and decorative illustrations with this technique, they lack his old vigour.

The same may be said of many of his line etchings. Where they depart least from his established style, as in 'Lady Dedlock in the Wood' (Plate 174), or 'The Stepping Stones' (Plate 193), with its evocation of the glare of the water and the cool darkness of the woods, they are at their most effective. The more spartan the line the greater the danger of insipidity unless the subject itself offers scope for the old indulgence in the grotesque, as in 'The Smallweed Family' (Plate 172), or the dramatic, as in 'The Consultation' (Plate 198).

If so much of his work at this time seems uninspired to modern eyes, it is simply that the material which he illustrated had little to inspire his demonstrable talents; and his work was further weakened by concessions to the new taste. Nor were these concessions enough to save him from appearing horribly old-fashioned to his contemporaries. He needed radically to alter his style as an artist to keep pace with 'High Art' and then to abandon etching and apply it to the woodcut if he was to hold his own with the artists of 'The 'Sixties Book'.

It is hard to say how heavily this weighted with Dickens—his publishers were doubtless far more aware of how old-fashioned Phiz had become—and was responsible for his decision to drop the artist after the thoroughly disappointing set of sixteen etchings which he provided for *A Tale of Two Cities* in 1859. It seems much more probable that Dickens was conscious that he himself had developed beyond the need for illustration of any kind, let alone the Hogarthian extension which Browne had supplied to the texts of the earlier novels. This would explain the absence of the sort of detailed instructions with which Browne had been bombarded and the virtual indifference with which Dickens treated his successors, Marcus Stone and Luke Fildes.[16]

If Dickens had outgrown Phiz, the process was probably gradual and the break may have been made easier for the novelist by the coldness between them which may well date back to the publication of *Little Dorritt* in 1857. John Harvey suggests that there is perhaps more than the usual nervous strain of writing in Dickens' request to W. H. Wills of 19 October 1855:

> Will you give my address (in Paris) to B[radbury] & E[vans] without loss of time, and tell them that although I have communicated at full explanatory length with Browne, I have heard *nothing of or from him*. Will you add that I am uneasy and wish they would communicate with Mr. Young, his partner, at once. . . .

Harvey also points out that, prior to the final break, Browne had told a Dr Carpenter of Croydon that his introduction would no longer carry much weight with Dickens, when the former was trying to get Dickens to address a local literary society. Harvey therefore suggests that when that break came in 1864 and Marcus Stone was commissioned to illustrate *Our Mutual Friend*, Browne was slightly disingenuous when, in writing to Young about Dickens' 'strangely silent manner of breaking the connection', he says:

> Marcus is no doubt to do Dickens. *I* have been a 'good boy', I believe. The plates in hand are all in good time, so I do not know what's 'up', any more than you. Dickens probably thinks a new hand would give his old puppets a fresh look, or perhaps he does not like my illustrating Trollope neck-and-neck with him—though, by Jingo, he need

> fear no rivalry *there*! Confound all authors and publishers, say I. There is no pleasing one or t'other. I wish I had never had anything to do with the lot.

Yet the break and the unkindly manner in which Browne conceived it had been made on Dickens' side left their scars. The illness, poverty and lack of recognition at the end of his life, by contrast with the fame of Dickens and the success which rightly or wrongly Browne and his family may have felt was due initially to the success of Browne's *Pickwick* plates, perhaps explain Edgar Browne's treatment of Dickens in his memoir of his father. The book's bitterness and its conscious effort to denigrate and belittle the novelist can be explained only by a festering grievance dating from this time.[17]

What made matters worse was the parting at about this time with other novelists with whom Browne had long been associated. Although in no sense Ainsworth's regular illustrator (he used a variety of artists), Browne had, after all, succeeded Cruikshank as the resident artist on *Ainsworth's Magazine* in 1844, had contributed a title-page and frontispiece to *Old St Paul's* (1847) and had illustrated *Revelations of London* (1844: *Auriol* 1865), *Crichton* (1849), *Mervyn Clitheroe* (1851–8), *The Spendthrift* (1857) and *Ovingdean Grange* (1860). However, with the exception of *Auriol* (which was the belated completion of a novel begun twenty years before), from 1861 Sir John Gilbert, and from 1865 his son, Frederick, were to illustrate the almost annual novel from Ainsworth. Furthermore, in the mid-1860s came the parting of the ways with Charles Lever. *Luttrell of Arran* was the last novel to be issued by Chapman & Hall, in 1865, Blackwoods becoming his regular British publishers (Lever himself contributed a regular column signed 'Cornelius O'Dowd' to *Blackwoods Magazine*); and Blackwoods did not publish illustrated fiction. Here at least Browne could take comfort from the fact that he had not been dropped by the author,[18] a fate he was to suffer in particularly humiliating circumstances soon after the break with Dickens.

Ironically it was the Anthony Trollope, of whom he had expressed such a low opinion, who inflicted this blow. When the novel which Browne mentions in his letter to Young, *Can You Believe Her?*, was half-way through its serial part-issue, Trollope abruptly dropped Browne and entrusted the rest of the illustrations to 'a lady'—Mary Ellen Edwards. The contrast between Browne's old-fashioned style and Miss Edwards' 'Sixties treatment is all the more marked since it is a contrast not between two novels by the same author but between two halves of the same novel. While by no means his best work, these are competent etchings and by any absolute standard Miss Edwards' illustrations are certainly not superior to them. However, where they scored in the eyes of Trollope and of his readers was that the figures in them are idealized and the black and white is the sharp effective contrast so successfully exploited by the wood-engravers of the 1860s. For not only had Browne's artistic style become out-dated but the medium of the etched steel-plate which he used to express it had been by now superseded by the woodcut.

In practical terms this meant a very considerable drop in income for him. John Harvey has estimated that for his Dickens illustrations (and the same scale must surely apply to his other etched work) Browne was paid for each steel-plate at rates which started in 1836 at £4, rising to £5 in 1841, to £6 6s by 1846, to £7 7s by 1850 and to £11 8s 6d in 1853. Although this fee would have had to be divided in some agreed proportion with Robert Young, it seems most probable that etching would have been more remunerative in terms of money, if not of time per design, than drawing for wood-engraving. Even from the incomplete evidence of the Check List we can see how his output of etched work fell during the decade 1851–60 to 430 designs—that is, to forty-three per annum as opposed to over sixty per annum in the earlier period—and, unlike that period, it seems certain that far fewer of the plates were etched in duplicate,[19] thus reducing still further the artist's income. Thomson states that it had fallen off when he moved farther out of London—from Thornton Heath to Banstead—but that the return to London in 1859 improved his finances, writing that 'he did a great deal of work, and in 1866 must have made a considerable income'.

This must have come from his great increased output of designs for wood-engraving. The books in the Check List give over 232 such designs for the period 1851–60, while for the period 1861–70 the figure is much the same, more than 227. (For comparison, in the latter period he etched only 122 plates, all before 1866.) However, these figures are deceptive, since they do not take into account his contributions to periodical publications[20] and a considerable body of designs for Routledge's Toy Books and other cheap juveniles which I have been unable to record.

Unfortunately much of this is hack-work and for this reason, and for others which will become apparent, it has tended to unbalance judgement of Browne's abilities as a designer for this medium, so that his son can write:

> Browne was an accomplished etcher, but he was never at home with the technique of woodcutting. He never seemed able to realise what changes an engraver might make in the appearance of his drawing. As a rule, the tendency was to increase the amount of white shown, and thereby thin the line, and also in free drawing to substitute something more mechanical. He never cured himself of using a mixed method of drawing and leaving the engraver to find his way out of it, which he generally did by cutting away anything that offered difficulty.

This is true of a great deal of the work produced in this medium from the mid-1850s—the illustrated editions of the novels of Fielding and Smollett published by Routledge in 1857, Ainsworth's *Ovingdean Grange* (1860) or novels by Horace Mayhew (1854), J. R. Ware (1860) and Mark Lemon (1864)—since these are cheap editions. Browne's designs depend on the one hand upon the amount which the engraver was prepared to put into cutting the block—Plates 180, 181, 194 and 202 show how Browne's talent can survive impairment by the engraver—and on the other upon a sympathy with his style which the engravers of the 1840s possessed but which their successors lacked, as Edgar Browne's remarks make plain.

Additionally, Browne's work in this period, and this is particularly true of his designs for children's books, suffers from the the method of reproduction. First of all his designs were presumbly printed not from wood-blcoks but from clichés,[21] to the detriment of his line, which then suffered the indignity of being overprinted in colour. This makes all the more hideous the hack-work done for Vickers—a series of cheap reprints which included *Peter Wilkins* (1860) and *Gulliver's Travels* and *Grimm's Goblins* (1861)—and can affect a book of much better quality, such as M. B. B. Edwards' *Snowflakes* (Plate 199). Although Browne was predominantly a black-and-white artist, *Home Pictures* (1850) shows how well he could design for tinted engravings, and *Dame Perkins and her Grey Mare* (1866) has equally charming lithographs made from Browne's water-colours. Yet the crux of the matter remains the sympathy with, and the care and skill which the engraver was prepared to devote to, his designs and their reproduction.

Perhaps as important a factor may be the opportunity for depicting congenial subject matter in the books which he was commissioned to illustrate. So many at this period are 'costume-pieces' (Ainsworth, Fielding, Smollett, Wharton's *Wits and Beaux* and even Dickens' *A Tale of Two Cities*) and Phiz was never happy as an historical artist. Drawing, as he did, from imagination, his characters look as if they belonged to a fancy-dress party rather than to real life. This can be seen in the set of early etchings to Pelham's *Chronicles of Crime*, in which contemporary mayhem is far more confidently and convincingly depicted than historic horrors. Notwithstanding, both in this and in the 1840 edition of Fielding's *Jonathan Wild* the illustrations of historical characters enjoy two substantial advantages: the designs come at first-hand from the artist's needle and do not suffer from the grey, perfunctory engraving of the later books; while the earlier books provide the scenes of low life and the strongly marked characters which Browne always found so congenial.

Even in the 1860s, when congeniality of subject is matched by care in reproduction, Browne could produce as good a series of designs for woodcuts as the twelve for what would seem to have been a Routledge Shilling Toy Book, *The Young Ragamuffin* (1866: Plates 207–9). The subjects are all low-life and when, as in this instance, the image is unimpared by overprinting in colour and is reproduced from india-paper proofs pulled from the actual wood-blocks, the results seem to give the lie to the claim that Browne was not at home designing for the woodcut. On the contrary, the London slum-life of the 1860s is just as powerfully evoked as the London of the Gordon Riots had been a quarter of a century before in the illustrations for *Barnaby Rudge*.

Indeed, the poor quality of so many of the woodcuts designed by Phiz in his later years cannot take away from the very successful designs he made for the wood-engravers in *Master Humphrey's Clock* in 1840–1. Nor is this an isolated instance. Although Browne was predominantly an etcher he also executed a large number of designs for wood, of which the chapter-openings to *The Confessions of Con Cregan* (1849: Plates 127, 129 and 130) are good examples both of his own and of the Romantic style in general. Nor should his contribution, minute though it was, to the Abbotsford Edition of the *Waverly Novels* be overlooked. This is a great Romantic Book and Browne's designs are well able to stand comparison with those of the doyen of French romantic book-illustration, Tony Johannot,[22] another of the artists who contributed to this illustrated edition of Scott's novels (Plates 54 and 92).

These three books are all in larger formats, and Browne showed his romantic affiliations and his abilities to design for wood-engraving best, perhaps, in the little books which are so pleasingly characteristic of the school. In France there was a great vogue in the early 1840s for the *Physiologies*, in which writers of the calibre of Balzac and artists of the ability of Daumier satirized the types and classes of contemporary society. They were immediately and directly imitated in England by Albert Smith's *Natural Histories*, and their influence can be seen in a whole series of smaller books for which Browne provided the designs for the woodcuts. They include *The Handbook of Swindling* (1839) *St Patrick's Eve* (1845: Plates 83 and 85), *A Romance of a Mince-pie* (1848: Plates 119 and 120), James Hannay's *Hearts are Trumps* and G. P. R. James's *The Fight of the Fiddlers* (both 1849), Lever's *Nuts and Nutcrackers* (1857) and Brough's *Ulf the Minstrel* (1859). Equally romantic in spirit are the woodcuts in the rather different books *Aunt Effie's Rhymes* (1852: Plates 164–8), *Agatha* (1861: Plate 159) and *Sir Guy de Guy* (1864: Plates 200 and 201), where careful and sympathetic wood-engraving combines with good paper and printing to do justice to Browne's designs.[23]

Browne's designs for woodcuts are in the Romantic tradition and the same may be said of his etchings. He is in the line of Hogarth, Rowlandson, Gillray and Cruikshank, whose satiric content and draughtsmanship influenced such French Romantic book-illustrators as Daumier and Gavarni. In fact the influence was reciprocal, Gavarni's work being well enough known in England for Albert Smith to write the text for his sketches of British life and character, *Gavarni in London*, while Daumier seems directly to have influenced Browne.[24] Sarah Gamp closely resembles a Daumier nurse and Browne adapted the Frenchman's Robert Macaire for his own illustrations to *Robert Macaire in England* (Plate 44). However, it was because he was a Romantic that Phiz fell from favour in the 1860s and thereafter had little opportunity to display his undoubted talent. We may deplore the hack-work, but must admire his courage in continuing to make his living as an artist.

This courage was even more neccessary and more admirable when disaster struck him in 1867. Browne himself made light of it, claiming that he was only suffering from severe rheumatism caught by sleeping in a draught during a seaside holiday, but it seems more than likely that illness was a form of polio contracted when bathing, since the immediate effects were almost total paralysis of the right side and blindness of the right eye. Although he gradually regained the use of his right fingers and partial use of his right leg, he had lost the sight of his right eye and was never able to use his right thumb again.

A lesser man would have been finished; but, although he still needed to use both hands to bring a glass to his lips, he insisted on being propped up at his table to draw, with the pencil between his fingers, until after half-an-hour he was forced to stop, exhausted and with the sweat dripping from him. Indomitably he struggled back to the grind of illustration and it seems incredible that, so short a time after what should have been a crippling illness, he could be producing work which is by no means despicable. *London's Great Outing* (1868: Plates 210 and 211) catches the atmosphere of the Derby which Browne had so often ridden over to Epsom to watch; *Sketches of the Seaside and the Country* (1869)[25] has all his old boisterous humour ('I'm on the Sea' (Plate 213) lurches sickeningly and effectively); while there is a crude vigour in the small woodcuts illustrating *All About Kisses* (1875: Plates 215 and 216).

But by now Browne had reached the end of the road and the wheel had come full circle. Once again he was dependent upon the sale of his watercolours and once more J. G. Fennell acted as his agent. Meanwhile the Dickens-collector, F. W. Cosens, nobly supported him with a commission to make watercolour drawings of all his Dickens plates. Further work was provided in the designs for the woodcuts to illustrate the Household Edition of Dickens and finally he prepared a hundred designs for similar illustrations to the Harry Lorrequer Edition of Lever's novels which Routledge published between 1876 and 1878. It would be pleasant to think of Phiz going out in a blaze of glory, but the watercolours are mechanical and the designs for the woodcuts such poor, crude things that it is hard to imagine they are by the same artist who etched the plates for the original editions of so many of the novels.

In July 1878 he was writing that 'things are as bad as they can be' and it was then, at the suggestion of his friends and with the assistance of his old partner, Robert Young, that he petitioned Disraeli for a Civil List pension. When this was refused and he had turned in vain to wealthy relatives for help, even his splendid optimism failed him, and on 15 March 1879 he wrote:

> I don't know where to turn or what to do. I have at last come to a full stop and don't see my way just yet to get on again. My occupation seems gone, extinct. I suppose I am thought to be used up, and I have been long enough before the public. I have not a single thing to do this year, nor for some months previous in the past year.

Yet help was at hand and it took a form which must have pleased Browne since it implied that, however the public viewed him, at least he was recognized by his fellow-artists. Thanks to the efforts of Frith, Fildes and Wells, the Royal Academy came to his aid with a small annuity. This enabled him to retire to Brighton, where he died on 8 July 1882, just four days short of his sixty-seventh birthday.[26]

His had been a full and productive life, enriched by a happy marriage and a very close family relationship. He had known early popularity and then neglect, but had met both success and failure with equanimity and crippling disease and acute pain with indomitable courage. Above all, he had preserved an integrity and an independence of mind. As his son wrote: 'His thoughts were entirely original. He had no idea of adopting anybody's opinions second-hand, but did not suppose that his own were of the slightest value or interest to anybody else.'

This modest obstinacy harmed him in his later years and may perhaps have prevented him from adapting his art to suit the taste of the 1860s.

Yet how productive he had been. In a working life of over forty years he had wholly or in part illustrated over two hundred books, for which he had etched about 1,500 original plates (and, in addition, provided duplicates for a large number of them), drawn over 1,100 designs for wood-engravings and produced innumerable watercolours and some oils as well. If neither so productive nor so great an artist as Cruikshank, he deserves to stand beside him as one of the foremost illustrators of the English Romantic Book and as one of the great book-illustrators of all time. In his collaboration with Dickens he achieved something so rare as to be perhaps unique. If the highest achievement of book-illustration is to balance exactly text and image, then his plates, the visual extension of the novelist's writing, do exactly this, and this modest craftsman has made his art a part of English literature.

Notes to Introduction

1 The *livre romantique* is the French manifestation of a European phenomenon and it is perfectly legitimate to apply to British books of the period and style the term 'Romantic Book' and to regard Browne as a Romantic artist.

2 Pronounced *Hab—lo*. There is no authority or logic for spelling the name *Hablôt*. See Edgar Browne: *Phiz and Dickens*, pp 1–3.

3 Bicknell (1788–1861) had taken Browne's sister Lucinda as his second wife in 1829. He was a leading figure in the whale-oil trade whose advice on economic matters was sought by governments of the day. A patron of contemporary British artists, he had formed a famous collection which was displayed at his house at Herne Hill. As a young man John Ruskin was a constant visitor and his enthusiasm for Turner was inspired by the paintings which Bicknell owned. Bicknell always seems to have taken a kindly interest in his brother-in-law and the Brownes were frequent visitors.

4 *The Life and Labours of Hablot Knight Browne* (1884)

5 *Hablot Knight Browne ('Phiz'). A Memoir* (1882)

6 Three per day was reckoned a fair stint. In fact Browne produced large numbers of watercolours throughout his life, mainly for his own amusement, but at the beginning and the end of his career from neccessity. This portion of his *oeuvre* does not fall within the scope of his study, but an adequate idea of the style of his domestic subjects is given by Plates 161–3 and that of his hunting pictures by Plates 205 and 206.

7 Browne was succeeded in June (probably on the recommendation of Dickens) by John Leech; but the magazine ran for only two more numbers (under a slightly changed name).

8 Dickens was, however, sufficiently impressed to bear Leech in mind for the future. On 5 November 1842 he could write:

> If it can possibly be arranged consistently with that regard which I feel bound to pay to Mr. Browne, I shall be truly happy to avail myself of your genius in my forthcoming Monthly Number [i.e., *Martin Chuzzlewit*].

But Browne objected to being replaced in this way and Leech's illustrations were confined to the *Christmas Books* (1843 onward).

9 He later wrote of the illustrations to *Jack Hinton*: 'Browne's sketches are as usual caricatures and make my scenes really too riotous and disorderly. The character of my books for uproarious people and incidents I mainly owe to Master Phiz.' At the time, a more serious complaint was that Harry Lorrequer too closely resembled Nicholas Nickleby (the novels were running neck-and-neck), and at the start of his career Browne did sometimes use stereotypes: his 'Poetical Young Gentleman' (Plate 17(b)) is a model for the poet Marchmont in Frances Trollope's *Charles Chesterfield*; and compare the horsewomen in Plates 17(a) and 49.

10 'Sir A—— E—— of D——'s', as Dickens wrote to John Forster.

11 As O'Connell's followers in the House of Commons were derisively styled.

12 Lever spent a year here (where Dickens visited him), and another at Como, before settling in Florence in 1848. Ten years later he became Vice-Consul at La Spezzia, before being promoted Consul at Trieste, where he died in 1872.

13 Browne was a keen horseman. The family claimed he would rather ride than walk fifty yards. He kept his horses at Croydon and regularly hunted with the local pack. His illustrations of horses are always good and, after his return to London (oddly enough), he published his sporting books *Hunting Bits* (1862) and *Racing and Chasing* (1868).

14 Typical is Kitton's anecdote:

> Phiz invariably depended upon his imagination or memory for his scenes and characters; as the artist expressed, he would merely go 'to have a look at a thing' and then be able to prepare his picture without further aid. For instance, before designing the weird illustration of 'The Lonely Figure' [Plate 177] in *Bleak House*, he visited a lime-pit, in order to see what the big crushing-wheels were like that he desired to introduce, and made a mental note of them without leaving the seat of his trap.
>
> (*Dickens and his Illustrators*)

15 At the start of Browne's career, fiction had been published either in monthly parts (e.g., Dickens and Lever) or in monthly instalments in literary periodicals (e.g., Ainsworth) before being issued in volume form. Such serials were normally illustrated by two plates per part and could run to as many as twenty parts (making forty plates in all). Although Chapman & Hall continued to publish in monthly parts (e.g., Lever and Trollope) until well into the 1860s, a new pattern of serialization in unillustrated journals developed, followed by three-volume publication (again without illustration). Subsequently a one-volume illustrated edition might be issued with a limited number of woodcut plates. Even had Browne's style found favour (which it did not), the actual number of plates per volume would have been greatly reduced.

16 Furthermore, Harvey, citing an article which Dickens wrote for *All the Year Round* (1869), demonstrates the novelist's lack of sympathy with the 'High Art' of the 'Sixties illustrators.

17 Notably his malignant description of one of Dickens' 'Penny Readings' and his acid remark that, 'The nation did not mourn because little Paul [Dombey] was dead, but because Mr. Dickens was so sorry.'

18 On the contrary Lever unsuccessfully attempted to persuade John Blackwood to employ Phiz. His letter to him on 14 June 1864 contains the following unconscious tribute to *St Patrick's Eve* and *Nuts and Nutcrackers*:

> I look forward to your promised letter about O'Dowd. No one could do an imaginary portrait of a foreignised Irishman—all drollery about the eyes, and

bearded like a pard—better than Hablot Browne (Phiz) and I think he could also do *all* that we need for illustration, which would be occasional bits on the page and tailpieces. If he would take the trouble to *read* the book (which he is not much given to), and if he would really interest himself in it (not so unlikely now, as he is threatened with a rival in Marcus Stone), he could fully answer all our requirements. I would not advise any regular 'plates', mere woodcuts in the page, and an occasional rambling one *crawling over* the page. What do *you* think?

19 This becomes very apparent in Johannsen's *Phiz.*

20 In the early part of his career Browne had contributed etchings and designs to literary and sporting periodicals (*Library of Fiction;* and *Ainsworth's, Union, The Illuminated, London* and *New Sporting Magazines*) and provided a cover for *Punch* in 1841. In the 1860s he contributed (at a lower level of art and of reproduction) to *The Illustrated Times, Once a Week, London Society* and *Judy,* and to the children's periodicals *Every Boy's Magazine* (Routledge) and *The Battle and the Breeze* (Vickers).

21 Harvey cites contemporary statements that the woodcut was longer-wearing than the steel-plate. Since the original steels were re-used as late as 1938 for the Nonesuch Dickens without apparent deterioration and since damage to woodblocks is a classic means of dating early printed books, this statement only makes sense if we assume printing not from the original blocks but from clichés taken from them.

22 The period of the *livre romantique* is said to have been inaugurated by his illustrations to Charles Nodier's *Le roi de Bohème et ses sept châteaux* (1830).

23 His illustrations to Rodwell's *Memoirs of an Umbrella,* designed at the height of his powers in 1845, turn out rather nasty because of the cheap production of the book.

24 Thackeray, in an article in *The London and Westminster Review* (1839), had advised him to study Daumier.

25 Illustrations in both these books are reproduced by Graphotype for, as Phiz wrote to his artist son, Walter, at this time:

> I am at (*present*) *on* a Sporting Paper . . . some of the Proprietors are Shareholders, &c., &c., in the Graphotype Co., so they want to work the two together.—I hate the process—it takes quite four times as long as wood—and I cannot draw and express myself with a nasty finishing brush, and the result when printed seems to alternate between something all as black as my hat—or as hazy and faint as a worn-out plate.

26 The cause of death was given as myelitis (inflammation of the spine), which seems to confirm that the illness of 1867 was, in fact, an attack of polio.

1 Hablot Knight Browne, 1815–82 (from a photograph)

1836: HENRY WINKLES, *Cathedral Churches of England and Wales*

2 'St Paul's, the South Front'

1836: [CHARLES DICKENS] *Sunday Under Three Heads*

3(a) Frontispiece

1838: [EDWARD CASWALL] *Morals from the Churchyard*

3(b) 'The Dying Beggar'

4 'Mr Wardle and his Friends under the Influence of the Salmon'

5 'First Appearance of Mr Samuel Weller'

6 'The Election at Eatanswill'

7 'Mr Pickwick and Sam in the Attorney's Office'

8 'The Middle-aged Lady in the Double-bedded Room'

9 'The Goblin and the Sexton'

10 Study for Mr Weller Senior

11 'The Valentine'

12 'Mr Winkle's Situation when the Door blew to'

13 'Mrs Bardell encounters Mr Pickwick in the Prison'

14 'Mr Bob Sawyer's Mode of Travelling'

15 Study for 'The Rival Editors'. Note how, in the finished etching (Plate 16 following), the rough sketch has been reversed and transformed from landscape to upright

16 'The Rival Editors'

1837: [EDWARD CASWALL] *Sketches of Young Ladies*

17(a) 'The Manly Young Lady'

1838: [CHARLES DICKENS] *Sketches of Young Gentlemen*

17(b) 'The Poetical Young Gentleman'

1838: JAMES GRANT, *Sketches in London*

18 'A Scene before the Curtain'

19 'Out-door Relief'

20 'Mr Ralph Nickleby's first Visit'

21 'The Internal Economy of Dotheboys Hall'

22 'Nicholas astonishes Mr Squeers and Family'

1839: CHARLES DICKENS, *Nicholas Nickleby*

23 'Theatrical Emotion of Mr Vincent Crummles'

24 Studies for the Cheeryble Brothers

25 'Linkinwater intimates his Approval of Nicholas'

26 ‘A sudden Recognition, unexpected on both sides’

27 'Great Excitement of Miss Kenwigs at the Hairdresser's Shop'

28 'The Children at their Cousin's Grave'

1839: CHARLES LEVER, *The Confessions of Harry Lorrequer*

29 'The supper at Father Malachi's'

30 'Lorrequer's debût at Strasburg'

31 Study for *Master Humphrey's Clock*. Note in Plate 32 (following) how Dickens' instructions have been carried out

32 Opening to 'The Clock' *The Old Curiosity Shop*

33 Opening to Chapter 6 (*The Old Curiosity Shop*)

34 Opening to Chapter 19 (*The Old Curiosity Shop*)

35 ‘Quilp and the Dog’ (*The Old Curiosity Shop*)

36 Opening to Chapter 38 (*The Old Curiosity Shop*)

37 'At Astley's Theatre' (*The Old Curiosity Shop*)

38 'Dick Swiveller and the Marchioness' (*The Old Curiosity Shop*)

39 'The Death of Quilp' (*The Old Curiosity Shop*)

40 Hugh (*Barnaby Rudge*)

41 'The No-Popery Dance' (*Barnaby Rudge*)

42 'Mr Gashford on the Leads' (*Barnaby Rudge*)

43 Gordon Rioters (*Barnaby Rudge*)

44 'Macaire addressing his Brethren in the Craft'

45 'John Smith Robbing a Hackney Coachman'

46 'An Irish Wake'

47 'Smith Stabbing a Policeman'

48 'The Rescue'

49 'The two Chestnuts'

50 'Shows how the Man of War kept watch'

51 'The Consultation in the Devil's Cavern'

52 'The Collision with the Prosperity'

53 'The Prosperity going down'

54 Tailpiece to *Guy Mannering* Chapter 2

55 'Job visited by a Master Tailor from Broadway'

56 'Godfrey's Interview with the Publisher'

57 'Hunting for Lodgings'

58 'Gregory taking his Gruel'

59 'Enid Waiting for her Husband'

60 'A Hunt after Tripe'

61 'Mr Fitzurse Horrified & terrified at the Approach of Mr Darius'

62 'The Finale to an evening'

(*Facing page*) 63 'Corny Delany'

embarkation within twenty-four hours. I begin half to despair of his being here in time. Should this be the case, will you, my dear Hinton, look after the old villain for me, at least until I write to you again on the subject?"

While I was yet pondering on these last few lines, I perceived that a card had fallen from my father's letter. I took it up, and what was my astonishment to find that it contained a correct likeness of Corny Delany, drawn with a pen, underneath which was written, in my cousin Julia's hand, the following few lines:—

"The dear old thing has waited three days, and I think I have at length caught something like him. Dear Jack, if the master be only equal to the man, we shall never forgive you, for not letting us see him.—Yours, JULIA."

This, of course, explained the secret of Corny's delay. My cousin, with her habitual wilfulness, preferring the indulgence of a caprice to any thing resembling a duty; and I now had little doubt upon my mind that O'Grady's fears were well founded, and that he had been obliged to sail without his follower.

The exertion it cost me to read my letters, and the excitement produced by their perusal, fatigued and exhausted me, and, as I sank back upon my pillow, I closed my eyes and fell sound asleep, not to awake until late on the following day; but strange enough, when I did so, it was with a head clear and faculties collected—my mind refreshed by rest, unbroken by a single dream: and so restored did I feel, that, save in the debility from long confinement to bed, I was unconscious of any sense of malady.

From this hour my recovery dated. Advancing every day with rapid steps, my strength increased; and, before a week elapsed, I so far regained my lost health, that I could move about my chamber, and even lay plans for my departure.

64 'St Senan's Well'

65 'Farewell to Tipperary Joe'

66 'Law and Physic in the Chamber of Death'

67 'A Slight Mistake'

68 'Denis promoted to the Dignity of a Horse'

69 'Meekness of Mr Pecksniff and his charming Daughter'

70 'Martin Chuzzlewit suspects the Landlady'

71 'Pinch starts homeward with the new Pupil'

72 'Truth prevails and Virtue is triumphant'

73 'Martin meets an acquaintance . . .'

74 'Mr Jefferson Brick proposes'

75 'The City of Eden . . . in Fact'

76 'Mr Pinch departs'

77 'Mr Jonas exhibits great Presence of Mind'

78 'Mrs Gamp propoges a Toast'

79 'Mr Pinch is amazed by a sudden apparition'

80 'The Nuptials of Miss Pecksniff'

81 'The Ruined House in the Vauxhall Road'

82 'The Compact'

It was late in the afternoon ere Owen was once more on the road down the mountain; for it was necessary—or at least believed so—that interment should take place on the day of death.

"I never thought it would be this way you'd go to your last home, father dear," said Owen aloud, and in a voice almost stifled with sobs; for the absence of all his friends and relatives at such a moment, now smote on the

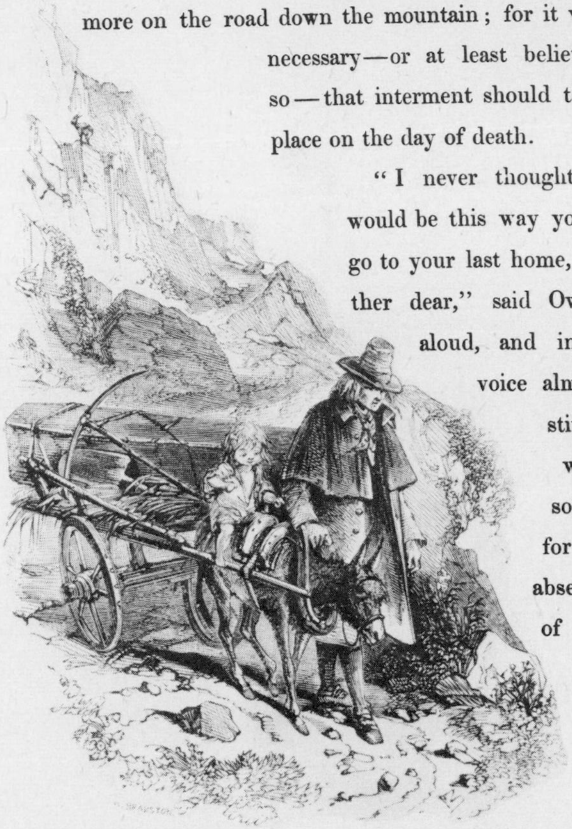

83 The Funeral of Owen's Father

84 'The Ambuscade'

stood, a vast procession could be seen moving on foot and on horseback. Some,

in country cars, assisted up the steep ascent by men's strong

P

85 The Mountain Path

86 Sketch for 'Sir Archy hears something to his Advantage' (see Plate 87 overleaf)

87 'Sir Archy hears something to his Advantage'

88 Sketch for 'The Escape'

89 'The Escape'

90 Sketch for 'Mark recognised by an old Acquaintance'.

91 'Mark recognised by an old Acquaintance'

92 Headpiece to *Woodstock* Chapter 17

93 'The Outcast Mother'

94 'Daly surveying the Robber's Imp'

95 'The Counsellor castigated'

96 Sketch for 'The Dombey Family'. Dickens accepted Browne's suggestion that the family should be portrayed seated, as in the plate following (97)

97 'The Dombey Family'

98 Sketch for 'Paul and Mrs Pipchin'

99 'Paul and Mrs Pipchin'. This was the illustration which so pained Dickens

100 'Dr Blimber's young Gentlemen . . .'

101 'Paul's Exercises'

102 Sketch for 'Major Bagstock is delighted . . .' Note the erasure of the figure of the Native, following Dickens' instruction that he should wear European, not Oriental dress

103 'Major Bagstock is delighted . . .'

104 'Solemn Reference is made to Mr Bunsby'

105 'Coming home from Church'

106 'A chance meeting'

107 'Florence and Edith on the Staircase'

108 'On the dark Road'

109 'Another Wedding'

1848: HABLOT K. BROWNE, *Four Plates to Illustrate the cheap Edition of The Old Curiosity Shop*

110 'The Marchioness'

111 'Paul'

112 Part of a sheet of preliminary studies for Mr Dombey

113 'Dombey'

114 'Henry and his facetious Landlady'

115 'The Close of a Night's Dissipation'

116 'The Sausage Party unexpectedly terminated'

117 'The Laboratory'

118 'The Descent of the Column'

Mr. Chirrup before leaving the shop did not look into the street, otherwise he would have seen a shabby hungry-like boy flattening his nose against one of the windows, and industriously contemplating the good things in them. This young gentleman had observed the mince-pie laid upon the counter, had marked the retreat of the master of the shop, and after waiting for a second to give him

law, sprung into the deserted warehouse, snatched up the coveted pasty, and was in the act of dis-

appearing over the threshold as Mr. Chirrup showed again at the glass door.

The flurried tradesman caught a momentary glimpse of an uplifted leg vanishing round his door-posts. His eye instinctively fell upon the counter: the mince-pie was gone. Mr. Chirrup was not given to gymnastics, but he vaulted into the public

The door was closed, the bolt was shot, the light vanished, and the drear wind of December howled amongst the leafless trees and over the insensible body of the murderer in mind, who lay motionless upon the stones.

CHAPTER V.

MEANTIME night crept slowly on, and the two good-hearted gossips, Mrs. Groats and Mrs. Tanks, still sat by the bed-side of poor Pattie. The girl had been, in their own phrase, "out of one fit into another" for hours, but these nervous struggles had gradually subsided, and the pastry-cook's niece had at length sunk into a sort of stupor, half doze, half faint.

121 'Impey amusing Hugh on his way to Minerva House'

(*Facing page*) 119 Mr Chirrup giving Case Chase

120 Tail piece to Chapter 4 and head piece to Chapter 5

122 'Please Ma'm can you tell me the way to—flare up'

123 'The Gunpowder Plot'

124 Sketch for 'Dolly Varden'

125 'Dolly Varden'

126 Engraved title-page to Volume 1

CHAPTER VI.

"VIEWS OF LIFE."

WHEN I woke the next morning, it was a few minutes before I could thoroughly remember where I was, and how I came there ; my next thought was the grateful one that if the calling was not a very exalted one, I had at least secured a mode of living, and that my natural acuteness, and better still, my fixed resolve within me "to get forward in the world," would not permit me to pass my days in the ignoble craft of a "horse-boy."

I found that the "walk," like every other career, had certain guiding rules and principles by which it was regulated. Not only were certain parts of the town interdicted to certain

127 Opening to Chapter 6

128 'A quiet Chop at "Kileen's"'

129 Opening to Chapter 18

CHAPTER XXVII.

"GUAJAQUALLA."

THERE are few things in this world gold cannot buy; but one among their number assuredly is—"a happy dream." Now, although I went to sleep in a great bed with damask hangings, and a gilt crown upon it, my pillow fringed with deep lace, my coverlet of satin edged with gold, I dreamed the whole night through of strifes, combats, and encounters. At one time my enemy would be an Indian; at another, a half-breed; now, a Negro; now, a jaguar, or a rattle-snake: but with whom, or whatever the struggle, it was always for money! Nothing else seemed to have any hold upon my thoughts. Wealth, and wealth alone, appeared the guiding principle of my being; and, as the penalty, I was now to learn the ceaseless anxieties, the torturing dreads, this passion begets.

With daylight, however, I awoke, and the bright sun streaming in, brought the glorious reality of my happy lot before me, and reminded me of the various duties my high state imposed. My first care was to ascertain the amount and

VOL. II. L

 Opening to Chapter 27

131 'The First Glimpse of the Legacy'

132 'The Ganger's Fate'

1850: CHARLES DICKENS, *David Copperfield*

133 Engraved title-page

134 'I am Hospitably received by Mr Peggotty'

135 'Changes at Home'

136 'Mrs Gummidge casts a damp on our Departure'

137 'My magnificent Order at the Public House'

138 and 139 Alternative sketches for 'I make myself known to my Aunt'

140 'I make myself known to my Aunt'

141 'Somebody turns up'

142 'Martha'

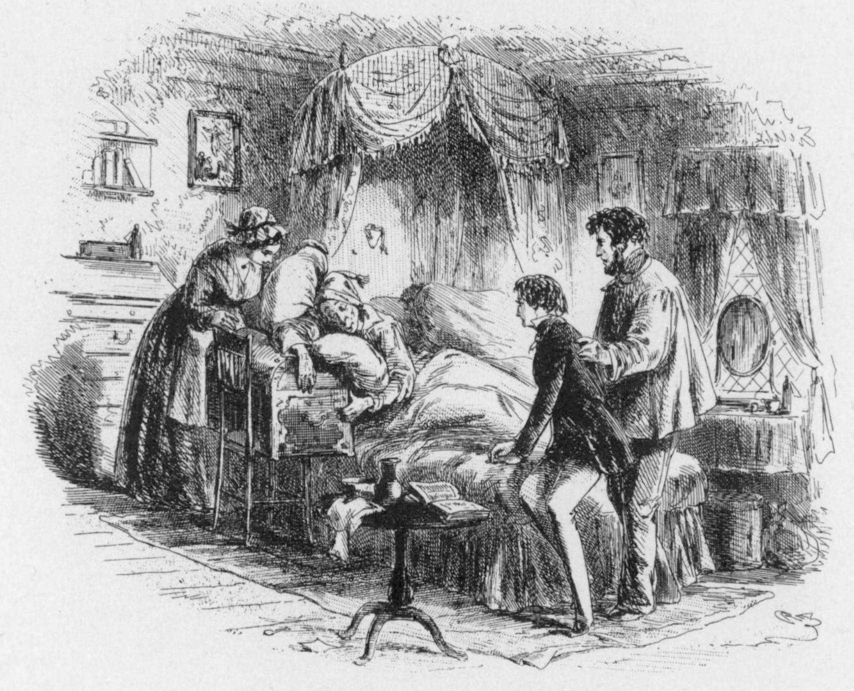

143 'Mr Barkis going out with the Tide'

144 'Mr Micawber delivers some valedictory Remarks'

145 'Our housekeeping'

146 'The River'

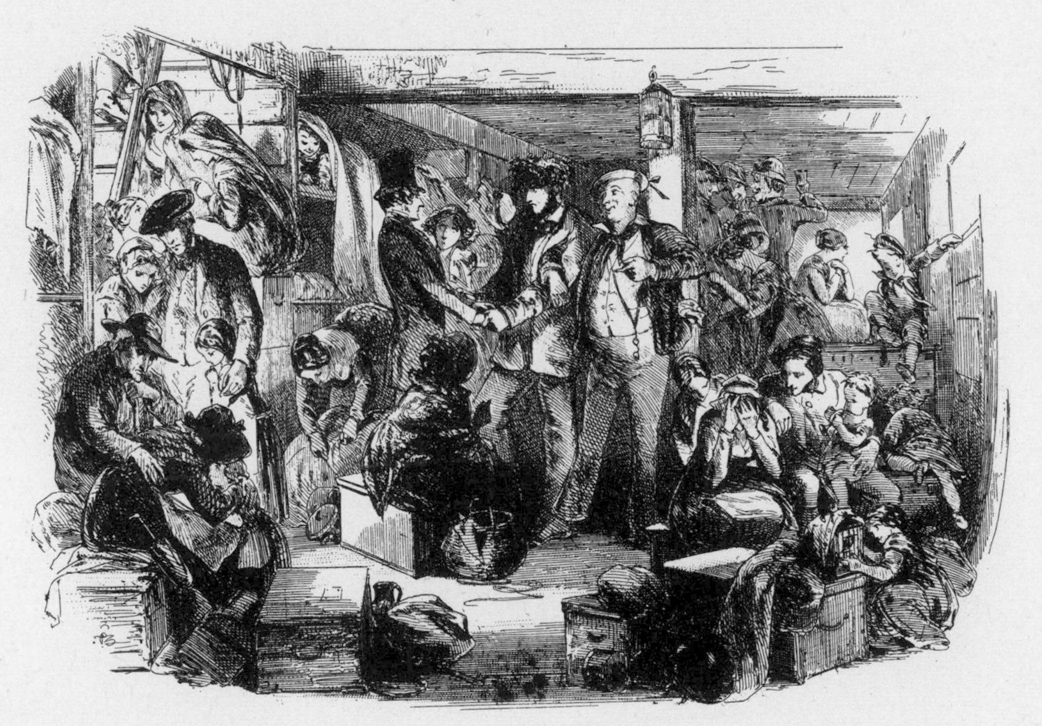

147 'The Emigrants'

148 'The Game at Monte'

149 'The Money Lender'

150 'A Domestic Detective'

151 'Corrigan parts with an old Friend'

1851: WILLIAM HARRISON AINSWORTH, *Mervyn Clitheroe*

MERVYN CLITHEROE

BY

W. HARRISON AINSWORTH.

LONDON & NEW YORK:

GEORGE ROUTLEDGE & SONS.

152 Engraved title-page

153 'My Adventure with the Gipsies'

154 'The Duel on Crabtree Green'

155 'The Stranger at the Grave'

156 'The Conjurers interrupted'

157 'I find Fournall in Conference with the Gipsies'

158 'The Deed of Settlement'

159 'The Black Guest of Drumgunniel'

160 'Margery Doyle and her Spouse'

(*above*) 161 'Night'

(*Facing page*) 162 'The Disjointed Nose' 163 'The Morning Bath'

THE CARPENTER'S SHOP.

I.

ONE morning, a spruce little Gimlet
Looked into a carpenter's shop;
And, standing upright on its screw,
It surveyed it from bottom to top.

164 'The Carpenter's Shop'

165 'The Little Mare'

GERTRUDE AND HER ALPHABET.

I.

OU have not heard the story yet
Of Gertrude and her Alphabet.
She learnt her letters from a board;
As yet, she could not read a word,
But stood beside her mother's knee,
Who pointed out great **A B C.**

166 'Gertrude and her Alphabet'

THE LITTLE BOY AND THE STARS.

II.

I am not happy lying here,
With neither book nor toy,
For I am sent to bed, because
I've been a naughty boy.

167 'The Little Boy and the Stars'

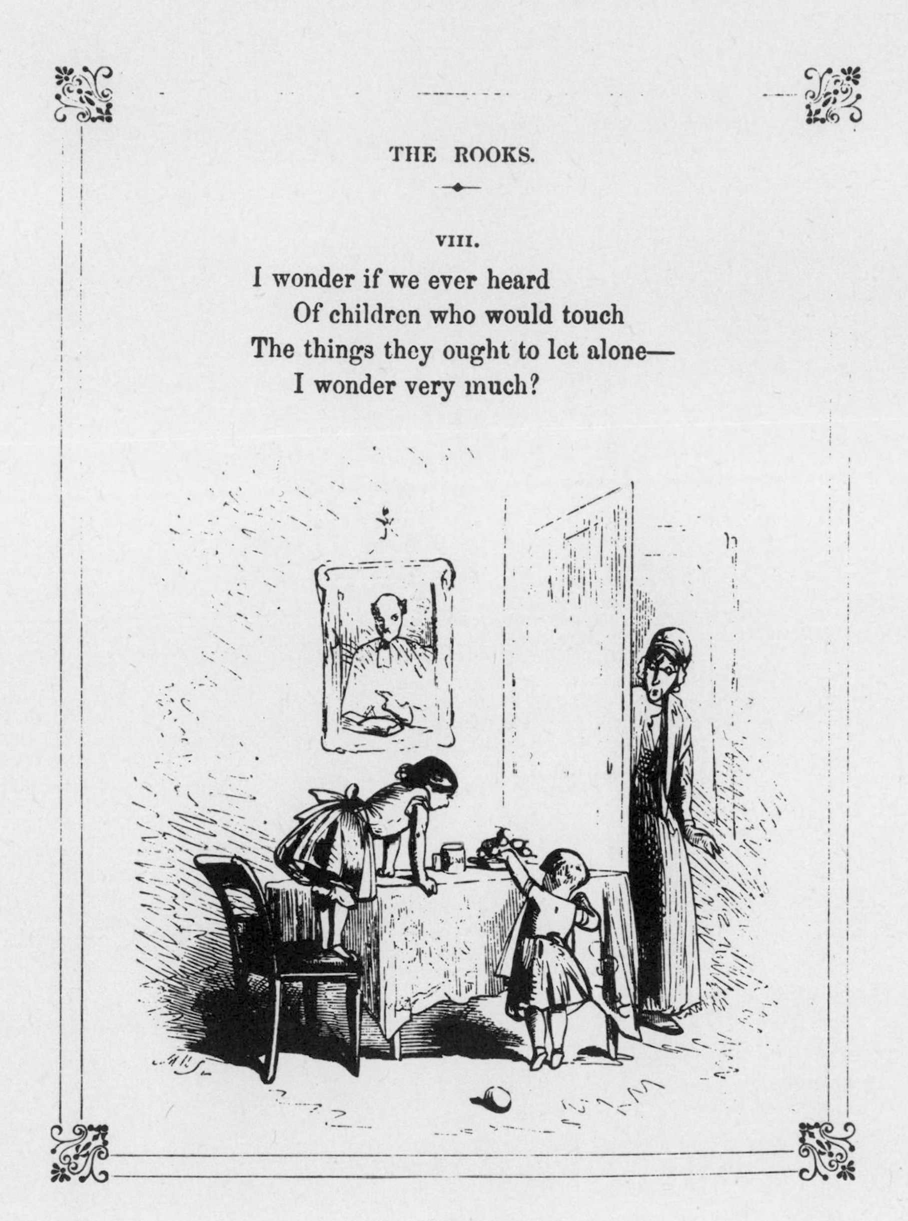

THE ROOKS.

VIII.

I wonder if we ever heard
Of children who would touch
The things they ought to let alone—
I wonder very much?

168 'The Rooks'

169 'Miss Jellyby'

170 'The Dancing School'

171 'Consecrated Ground'

172 'The Smallweed Family'

173 'Mr Chadband improving a tough subject'

174 'Lady Dedlock in the Wood'

175 'Tom All Alone'

176 'Shadow'

177 'The Lonely Figure'

178 'The Night'

179 'The Morning'

180 'Pomp and Vanity'

181 'The Fright in the Wood'

182 'Making Off'

183 'Mr F's Aunt is conducted into Retirement'

184 'Little Dorritt's Party'

185 'The Ferry'

186 'The Brothers'

187 'Visitors at the Works'

188 'The Third Volume of the Register'

189 'The Asylum for the Houseless'

190 'The Meeting at Stonehenge'

191 'The Pony Race'

192 'The Revd Paul returning with Dispatches'

193 'The Stepping Stones'

194 Frontispiece

Roland.

T was Christmas time, and it was night. A full moon rode the cloudless heavens, and gave back so gloriously the lustre she borrowed that even Shadow, shrinking behind gables and into rifts and pits, seemed but a diminished degree of light, for light was everywhere. The most noisome pool, the most pestilent matter, caught the pure beam, and gave

195 Opening to 'Roland'

196 'Magdalene'

197 'The Major "departs" but not in "peace"'

198 'The Consultation'

Alas! he has no home but ours,
No other parents but us two;
The secret of his name and birth
Beneath the waves is buried low."

In that home so rough and wild,
Happy was the foundling child;
Books nor toys nor games had he,
Playmates were the rocks and sea,

To them he prattled, laughed and sung,
Merrily, merrily, all day long.

21

199 A page of text

Would such impetuous wooing stand,
And not with anger swell?
Her hand descends upon his ear:
Off flies his cap, and—bang! oh dear,
She scalps him clean! for disappear
His hat and hair as well!

"Down, down, sir, on your bended knees!
My pardon ask! How dare you seize
My favours by such means as these?
I will my father tell!"

As cause is followed by effect,
What consequence should you expect,
When mortal hand assaults the ear
Of any British Volunteer?

“And how shall I convey my things?”
  “A bandbox, love, is all you need.”
“’Tis ready!” “Cord it well with strings.”
  “’Tis done! Go fetch the female steed!”

Arcadian frankness! . . . Guy, of course,
  Bounds like an antelope away;
Returning quickly with the horse
  Of gentle sex and colour grey.

201 The Elopement

202 'Recollections of a retired Butler'

(*Facing page*) 203 Engraved title-page

1865: CHARLES LEVER, *Luttrell of Arran*

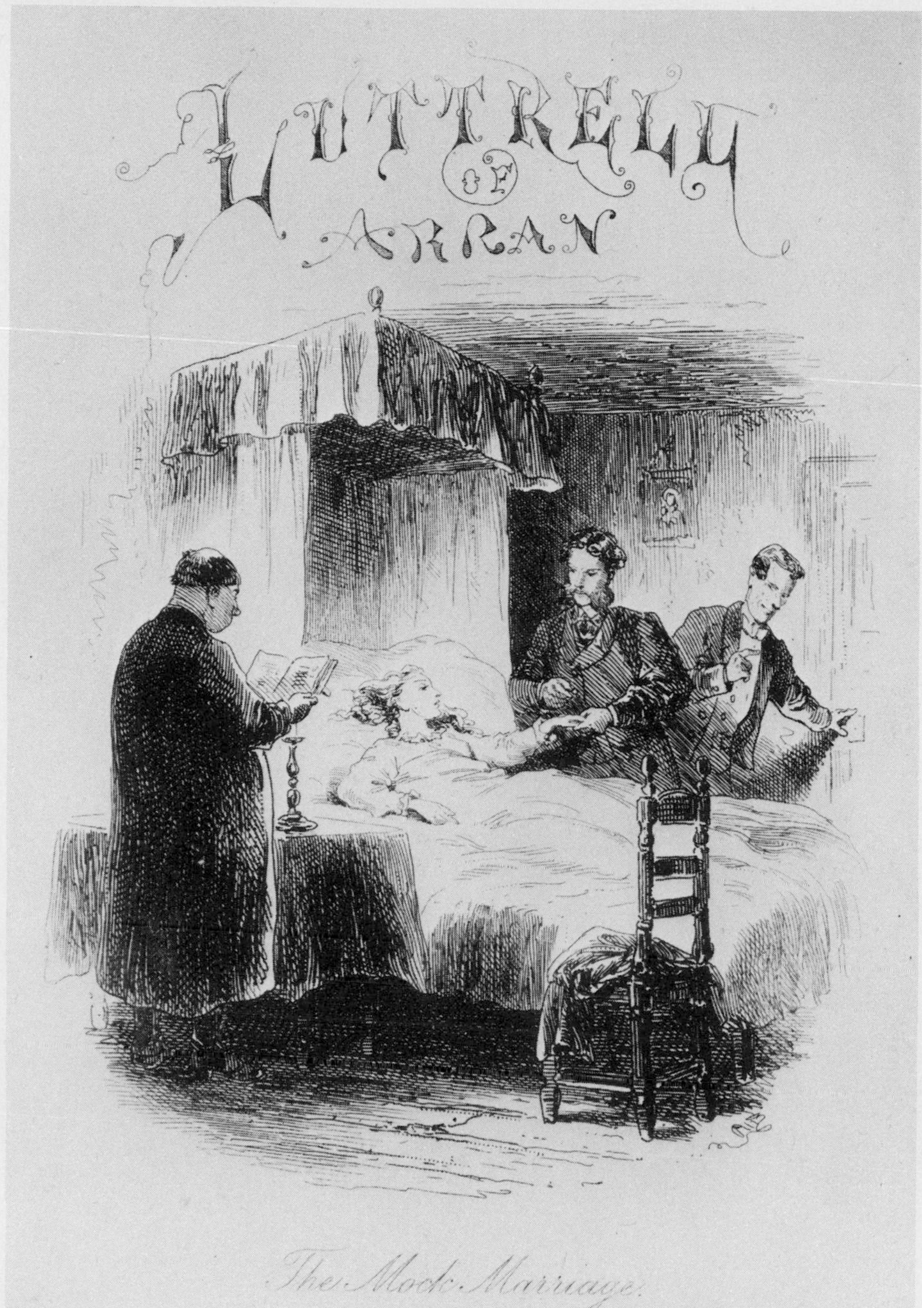

204 'The Letter'

205 'Dame Perkins about to Start'

206 'Hark forward!'

207 An India-paper Proof

1866: [ANONYMOUS], *The Young Ragamuffin*

208 An India-paper Proof

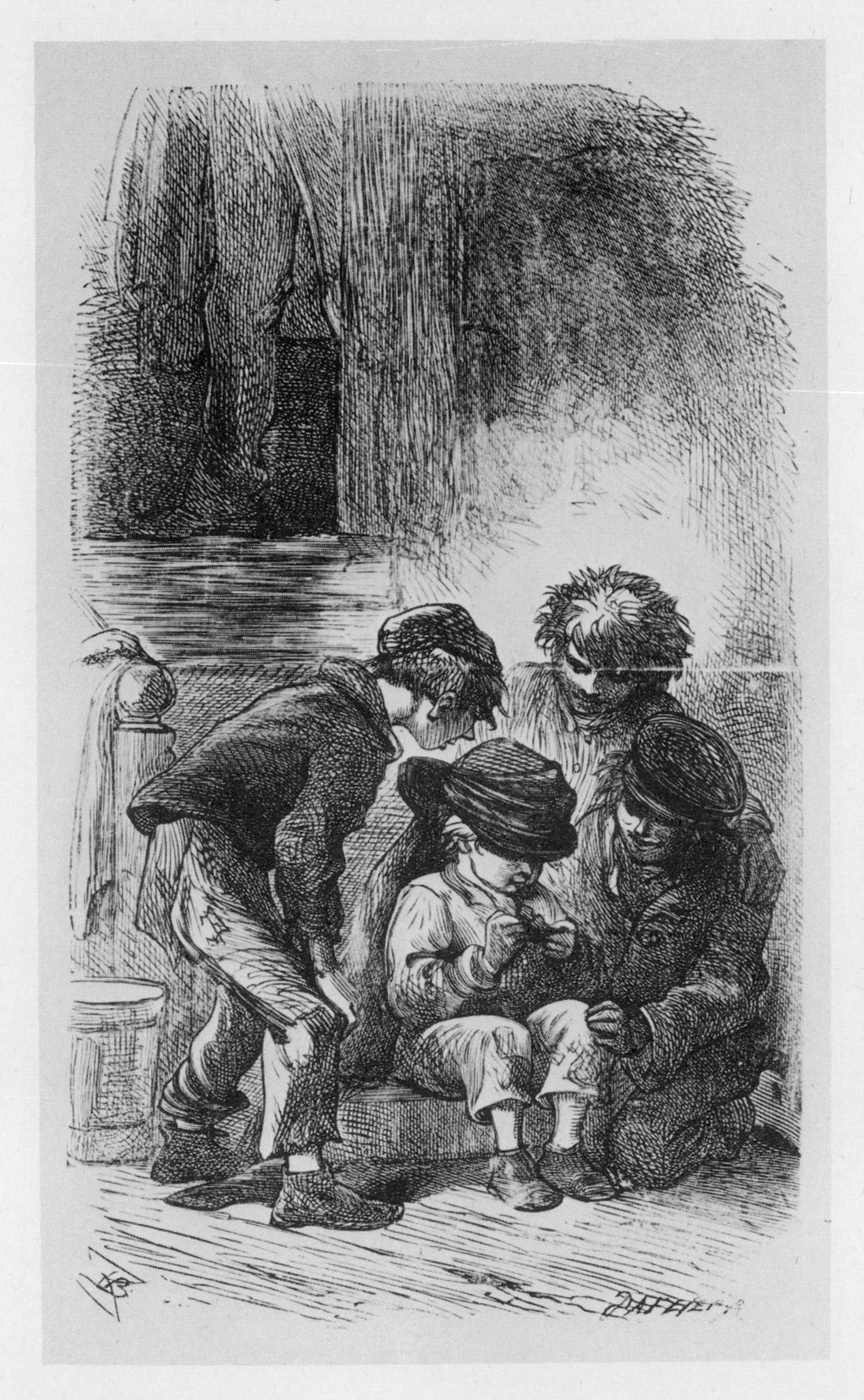

209 An India-paper Proof

210 Derby Crowd

211 On the road home

212 'Busy Builders'

213 'I'm on the Sea'

"Goodness only knows!" sighed Mr. Popham. "I got into a field, and I thought I should never find my way out."

OUR HERO AND HIS FRIEND POPHAM SUDDENLY CONFRONT EACH OTHER.

"How very curious," said Mr. Samuel, moralizing on the coincidence. "Why, I got into a field, and thought I should never be able to get out."

214 'Our Hero and his friend Popham suddenly confront each other'

88

He fumbles up into a loose adieu ;
And scants us with a single famish'd kiss,
Distasted with the salt of broken tears."

"O, the kindest Kate !—
She hung about my neck ; and kiss on kiss
She vied so fast, protesting oath on oath,
That in a twink she won me to her love."

TAMING OF THE SHREW, act ii. sc. I.

" *Katharina.*—Husband, let's follow, to see the end of
Pet.—First kiss me, Kate, and we will. [this ado.

215 Kissing in the Street

150

"For soon I led the yielding fair
By gentlest words, and tend'rest care,
From granting first a sidelong kiss,
To the more dear delightful bliss,
With which the melting soul's replete
When lips meet lips in kisses sweet!"

"'I'll scream if you touch me!'
Exclaimed a pert miss,
Whose lover was seeking
An innocent kiss.

By this prudish conduct
Cold water was thrown;
The lover drew backward
And let her alone.

216 'I'll scream if you touch me'

see John Hassall's opinion p28 in McLean

Check List of Books Illustrated by Hablot Knight Browne

Books with woodcut illustrations marked*
Books to which Browne contributed illustrations marked†

1836
[Charles Dickens]: *Sunday Under Three Heads**
Henry Winkles: *Cathedral Churches of England and Wales* Vol I†

1837
[Edward Caswall]: *Sketches of Young Ladies*
Charles Dickens: *Posthumous Papers of the Pickwick Club*†

1838
E[dward] C[aswall]: *Morals from the Churchyard**
[Charles Dickens]: *Sketches of Young Gentlemen*
James Grant: *Sketches in London*
S. Oliver: *The Old English Squire*
R. S. Surtees: *Jorrocks' Jaunts and Jollities*
Henry Winkles: *Cathedral Churches of England and Wales* Vol II†

1839
Charles Dickens: *Nicholas Nickleby*
'Joseph Fume': *A Paper of Tobacco*
Charles Lever: *Harry Lorrequer*
J. P. Robertson: *Solomon Seesaw*
'Captain Barabbas Whitefeather': *The Handbook of Swindling**

1840
[Anon]: *The Legend of Cloth Fair*
[Charles Dickens]: *Sketches of Young Couples*
Henry Fielding: *Jonathan Wild*
T. E. Hook: *Precepts and Practice*
G. W. M. Reynolds: *Robert Macaire in England*

1841
Charles Dickens: *Master Humphrey's Clock**†
Charles Dickens (editor): *The Pic-nic Papers*†
T. E. Hook: *Peter Priggins*
Charles Lever: *Charles O'Malley*
W. J. Neale: *Paul Periwinkle*
'Cavendish Pelham': *Chronicles of Crime*[1]
Frances Trollope: *Charles Chesterfield*

1842
Cornelius Mathews: *The Career of Puffer Hopkins*
W. H. Maxwell: *Rambling Recollections of a Soldier of Fortune**
G. T. Miller: *Godfrey Malvern*
Sir Walter Scott: *Waverley Novels* (Abbotsford Edition) Vol I*†

1843
William Carleton: *Traits and Stories of the Irish Peasantry*†
G. P. R. James: *The Commissioner*[2]
Charles Lever: *Our Mess* (Vol I *Jack Hinton the Guardsman**: Vols II and III *Tom Burke of Ours*)

1844
W. H. Ainsworth: *Revelations of London*[3]
Charles Dickens: *Martin Chuzzlewit*
George Raymond: *The Memoirs of R. W. Elliston*†

1845
[Anon]: *Fiddle Faddle's Sentimental Tour*
Charles Lever: *The O'Donoghue*
Charles Lever: *St Patrick's Eve**
G. H. Rodwell: *Memoirs of an Umbrella**

1846
William Carleton: *Valentine McClutchy*
'Democritus': *Medical and Christian Dissection of Teetotalism*
Charles Rowcroft: *Fanny the Little Milliner*
Sir Walter Scott: *Waverley Novels* (Abbotsford Edition) Vol X*†

1847
W. H. Ainsworth: *Old St Paul's*†
[Anon]: *Longlost Found*
Charles Lever: *The Knight of Gwynne*
John Smith: *Irish Diamonds**
R. S. Surtees: *Hawbuck Grange*

1848
H. K. Browne: *Dombey and Son, the Four Portraits*
H. K. Browne: *Dombey and Son, Full-length Portraits*
H. K. Browne: *Four Plates to illustrate the cheap edition of 'The Old Curiosity Shop'*
Daniel Defoe: *Robinson Crusoe**
Charles Dickens: *Dombey and Son*
W. B. Jerrold: *The Disgrace to the Family*
Augustus and Horace Mayhew: *The Image of his Father*
A. B. Reach: *The Romance of a Mince-Pie**

1849
W. H. Ainsworth: *Crichton*
H. K. Browne: *Four Plates to illustrate the cheap edition of 'Barnaby Rudge'*
James Hannay: *Hearts are Trumps**
G. P. R. James: *The Fight of the Fiddlers**
Charles Lever: *The Confessions of Con Cregan**
Bulwer Lytton (Frontispiece to *Eugene Aram*)
Albert Smith: *The Pottleton Legacy*

1850
Charles Dickens: *David Copperfield*
Charles Lever: *Roland Cashel*
Samuel Lover: *Metrical Tales**†
Bulwer Lytton (Frontispieces to four novels)

1851
W. H. Ainsworth: *Mervyn Clitheroe*[4]
H. K. Browne: *Home Pictures*
S. Le Fanu: *The Fortunes of Colonel Torlogh O'Brien*
S. Le Fanu: *Ghost Stories*
Bulwer Lytton (Frontispieces to three novels)

1852
[Anon]: *Aunt Effie's Rhymes for Children**
H. K. Browne: *Illustration of the Five Senses*
Charles Lever: *The Daltons*
Bulwer Lytton: (Frontispieces to two novels)
J. C. Maitland: *The Doll and her Friends**
F. E. Smedley: *Lewis Arundel*

1853
William Carleton: *Traits and Stories of the Irish Peasantry**
Charles Dickens: *Bleak House*
Bulwer Lytton: (Frontispieces to three novels)
F. E. Smedley: *The Fortunes of the House of Colville*

1854
Lord Byron: *Poetical Works**†
Lady Pamela Campbell: *The Cabin by the Wayside**
'Christian Le Ros': *Christmas Day**
Charles Lever: *The Dodd Family Abroad*
Bulwer Lytton (Frontispieces to two novels)
Horace Mayhew: *Letters left at a Pastry-cook's**
F. E. Smedley: *Harry Coverdale's Courtship*
A. E. Stothard: *A Peep at the Pixies**

1855
Mary and Elizabeth Kirby: *The Discontented Children**

1856
Charles Lever: *The Martins of Cro-Martin*

1857
W. E. Ainsworth: *The Spendthrift**
H. K. Browne: *Merry Pictures**†
Charles Dickens: *Little Dorritt*
Henry Fielding: *Amelia**
Henry Fielding: *Joseph Andrews**
George Halse: *Queen Loeta and the Mistletoe*
[Charles Lever]: *Nuts and Nutcrakers**
Augustus Mayhew: *Paved with Gold*
Tobias Smollett: *Humphrey Clinker**
Tobias Smollett: *Peregrine Pickle**

1858
[Anon]: *Aunt Mavor's Third Book of Nursery Rhymes**
[Anon]: *Christmas Cheer**
Mrs Gatty: *Legendary Tales**
G. W. Thornbury: *The Buccaneers**

1859
R. Brough: *Ulf the Minstrel**[5]
Charles Dickens: *A Tale of Two Cities*
Charles Lever: *Davenport Dunn*
Mrs H. B. Stowe: *The Minister's Wooing*

1860
W. H. Ainsworth: *Ovingdean Grange**
H. Caldwell: *The Art of Doing Our Best**
Robert Paltock: *The Adventures of Peter Wilkins**

J. R. Ware: *The Fortunes of the House of Pennyl**
'G. and P. Wharton': *Wits and Beaux of Society**
1861
[Anon]: *Confessions of a Page**
[Anon]: *Grimm's Goblins**
[Anon]: *New Mysteries of London**
George Halse: *Agatha**
Charles Lever: *One of Them*
H. C. Pennell: *Puck on Pegasus**†
Jonathan Swift: *Gulliver's Travels**
1862
H. K. Browne: *Hunting Bits*
M. B. B. Edwards: *Snowflakes**
Charles Lever: *Barrington*
1864
Maria Edgeworth: *The Parents' Assistant**
[George Halse]: *Sir Guy de Guy**
Mark Lemon: *Tom Moody's Tales**
C. H. Ross: *The Strange Adventure of Two Single Gentlemen**†
Anthony Trollope: *Can you forgive her?*†
1865
Charles Lever: *Luttrell of Arran*
R. S. Surtees: *Mr Romford's Hounds*†
1866
[Anon]: *The Young Ragamuffin**
Thomas Hood: *Penny Readings**
L. Meadows: *Dame Perkins and her Grey Mare*
1867
[Anon]: *Ghost Wives**
1868
H. K. Browne: *London's Great Outing*[6]
H. K. Browne: *Racing and Chasing*
1869
H. K. Browne: *Sketches of the Seaside and the Country*
1871
'M. Legrand': *The Cambridge Freshman**
1875
'Damocles': *All About Kisses**
1876
Charles Lever: *Novels* (Harry Lorrequer Edition) Vols I–X*
1877
Charles Lever: *Novels* (Harry Lorrequer Edition) Vols XI–XXI*
1878
Charles Lever: *Novels* (Harry Lorrequer Edition) Vols XXII–XXXI*
1882
George Halse: *A Salad of Stray Leaves*[7]
William Shakespeare: *Works**†
1883
H. K. Browne: *Phiz's Baby Sweethearts**[8]
H. K. Browne: *Phiz's Funny Alphabet**
H. K. Browne: *Phiz's Funny Stories**
H. K. Browne: *Phiz's Merry Hours**
1890
[Anon]: *The Frog would a'wooing go*†[9]

Notes to Check List

1 A selection of these plates was used to illustrate L. Benson's *Book of Remarkable Trials* (1871).
2 Twenty of the plates were retitled and used to illustrate *Samuel Sowerby* (1845).
3 Eventually completed and published as *Auriol* in 1865.
4 Eventually completed and published in 1858.
5 Reissued in *The Little Red Man* (1870).
6 Folio: reissued the following year as *The Derby Carnival* in quarto.
7 The frontispiece is the last item of book-illustration executed by Browne. Halse had been a consistent patron of his work.
8 These four titles are very probably re-issues of work done for Routledge in the 1850s and published anonymously. Browne's death in 1882 and the consequent revival of interest in him would have persuaded the publishers that it was worth cashing in on his name in this way.
9 A reissue of 1850s illustration. Like all publishers, Routledge rang the changes on their stock of blocks and these would have appeared in such nursery-rhyme collections as Mother Goose and the Aunt Mavor series.

Index of Plates

1849: ALBERT SMITH, *The Pottleton Legacy*

131 'The First Glimpse of the Legacy'
132 'The Ganger's Fate'

1850: CHARLES DICKENS, *David Copperfield*

133 Engraved title-page
134 'I am Hospitably received by Mr Peggotty'
135 'Changes at Home'
136 'Mrs Gummidge casts a damp on our Departure'
137 'My magnificent Order at the Public House'
138, 139 Alternative sketches for 'I make myself known to my Aunt'
140 'I make myself known to my Aunt'
141 'Somebody turns up'
142 'Martha'
143 'Mr Barkis going out with the Tide'
144 'Mr Micawber delivers some valedictory Remarks'
145 'Our housekeeping'
146 'The River'
147 'The Emigrants'

1850: CHARLES LEVER, *Roland Cashel*

148 'The Game at Monte'
149 'The Money Lender'
150 'A Domestic Detective'
151 'Corrigan parts with an old Friend'

1851: WILLIAM HARRISON AINSWORTH, *Mervyn Clitheroe*

152 Engraved title-page
153 'My Adventure with the Gipsies'
154 'The Duel on Crabtree Green'
155 'The Stranger at the Grave'
156 'The Conjurers interrupted'
157 'I find Fournall in Conference with the Gipsies'
158 'The Deed of Settlement'

1851: SHERIDAN LE FANU, *The Fortunes of Colonel Torlogh O'Brien*

159 'The Black Guest of Drumgunniel'
160 'Margery Doyle and her Spouse'

1851: HABLOT K. BROWNE, *Home Pictures*

161 'Night'
162 'The Disjointed Nose'
163 'The Morning Bath'

1852: [ANONYMOUS], *Aunt Effie's Rhymes for Children*

164 'The Carpenter's Shop'
165 'The Little Mare'
166 'Gertrude and her Alphabet'
167 'The Little Boy and the Stars'
168 'The Rooks'

1853: CHARLES DICKENS, *Bleak House*

169 'Miss Jellyby'
170 'The Dancing School'
171 'Consecrated Ground'
172 'The Smallweed Family'
173 'Mr Chadband improving a tough subject'
174 'Lady Dedlock in the Wood'
175 'Tom All Alone'
176 'Shadow'
177 'The Lonely Figure'
178 'The Night'
179 'The Morning'

1854: HORACE MAYHEW, *Letters left at a Pastrycook's*

180 'Pomp and Vanity'

1855: MARY and ELIZABETH KIRBY, *The Discontented Children*

181 'The Fright in the Wood'

1857: CHARLES DICKENS, *Little Dorritt*

182 'Making Off'
183 'Mr F's Aunt is conducted into Retirement'
184 'Little Dorritt's Party'
185 'The Ferry'
186 'The Brothers'
187 'Visitors at the Works'
188 'The Third Volume of the Register'

1857: AUGUSTUS MAYHEW, *Paved With Gold*

189 'The Asylum for the Houseless'
190 'The Meeting at Stonehenge'

1857–9: CHARLES LEVER, *Davenport Dunn*

191 'The Pony Race'

192 'The Revd Paul returning with Dispatches'

193 'The Stepping Stones'

1858: MRS GATTY, *Legendary Tales*

194 Frontispiece

1861: GEORGE HALSE, *Agatha*

195 Opening to 'Roland'

196 'Magdalene'

1862: CHARLES LEVER, *Barrington*

197 'The Major "departs" but not in "peace"'

198 'The Consultation'

1862: M. B. B. EDWARDS, *Snowflakes*

199 A page of text

1864: [GEORGE HALSE], *Sir Guy de Guy*

200 Dismissal

201 The Elopement

1864: MARK LEMON, *Tom Moody's Tales*

202 'Recollections of a retired Butler'

1865: CHARLES LEVER, *Luttrell of Arran*

203 Engraved title-page

204 'The Letter'

1866: LINDON MEADOWS, *Dame Perkins and her grey Mare*

205 'Dame Perkins about to Start'

206 'Hark forward!'

1866: [ANONYMOUS], *The Young Ragamuffin*

207–209 Three India-paper Proofs

1868: PHIZ, *London's Great Outing*

210 Derby Crowd

211 On the road home

1869: PHIZ, *Sketches of the Seaside and the Country*

212 'Busy Builders'

213 'I'm on the Sea'

1871: [JAMES RICE], *The Cambridge Freshman*

214 'Our Hero and his friend Popham suddenly confront each other'

1875: DAMOCLES, *All About Kisses*

215 Kissing in the Street

216 'I'll scream if you touch me'

Index